STENCILS AND
STENCILLING

WENDY CRAIG

ACKNOWLEDGEMENTS

Working on this book has been more pleasure than pain and I would like to thank all those at Struik who have led me through this first endeavour – especially Linda de Villiers, Cecilia Barfield and Bev Dodd. Thanks also to Warren Heath and Mike Calitz who produced the stunning pics and to Sonya Nel who styled the photographs so beautifully.

Grateful thanks to Plascon Paints and Crisitex, which generously supplied products for me to experiment with, and to Lucille Riordin of Waltons, Somerset West, and Linda Rose of Crafter's Inn, Somerset West, for the loan of their products for the photographs.

Karen Peters and Charmian Newton-Foot shared their knowledge of ceramics to help me in a field that was entirely new. Thanks to Ruth Hall who painstakingly put all the stencil designs onto computer.

For permission to photograph the beautiful stencilling on their premises I would also like to thank Simonsberg Cheese, Stellenbosch (cover and page 4), Europa Coffee Shop, Hermanus (pages 28 and 29) and The Hout Bay Manor Hotel, Hout Bay (page 105).

Published by Struik Publishers (a division of New Holland Publishing (South Africa) (Pty) Ltd)

New Holland Publishing is a member of Johnnic Communications Ltd

Cornelis Struik House, 80 McKenzie Street, Cape Town 8001

86 Edgware Road, London, W2 2EA, United Kingdom

14 Aquatic Drive, Frenchs Forest, NSW 2086, Australia

218 Lake Road, Northcote, Auckland, New Zealand

www.struik.co.za

Publishing manager: Linda de Villiers

Editor: Cecilia Barfield

Designer: Bev Dodd

Photographer: Warren Heath

Stylist: Sonya Nel

Proofreader: Helen de Villiers

Reproduction: Hirt & Carter Cape (Pty) Ltd

Printing and binding: Sing Cheong Printing Company Limited

ISBN 1 86872 968 0

10 9 8 7 6 5 4 3 2 1

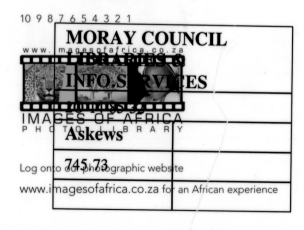

CONTENTS · CONTENTS

CONTENTS · CONTENTS

Stencilling has been around as far back as when man lived in caves and recorded details of his everyday life. Proof that almost every early civilisation throughout the world used stencils abounds and can be seen today in the Palaeolithic cave paintings dating from 30 000 BC to early Australian Aboriginal stencils from 4 000 years ago, which were recently discovered in the Wollemi National Park in New South Wales.

Since 8 000 BC, stencils were used extensively in China where they were cut from varnished mulberry fibres. Silk threads held intricate stencils together, which resulted in such a fine print that the bridges were almost invisible and, in reality, heralded the beginning of the art of silk-screening.

The ancient Egyptians used stencils in the decoration of tombs in the pyramids, as a pattern for low relief work. Before they came into contact with Western civilisation, even the Inuit people of north America made stencils cut from sealskin. Traditionally, stencils made from materials as diverse as bamboo and banana leaves were used in the Fijian Islands but, because of their organic nature, have long since perished.

Many cultures use stencilling to resist-dye fabrics. In Africa, stencilling has long been a major form of resist-dyed adire textile decoration among the Yoruba people of Nigeria. They use corrugated roof sheeting that is hammered flat, after which the stencil is cut into the metal with a chisel. Cutting of the stencil is men's work, while women apply starch through the stencil with a pliable metal spatula and the cloth is then dyed once the starch is dry. The cloth is washed repeatedly until all the starch is removed and the stencil design revealed.

Barkcloth stencils are also used by the Ganda people of East Africa, who use banana leaves for the stencil and then apply a black paste of vegetable dye and mud to decorate the fabric.

I was most fascinated to discover how extensively stencilling has been used in South Africa – from the cave paintings of the San peoples to the 18th century Cape Dutch mansions of the early settlers. Few examples of these early wall decorations have survived but some can still be seen at places such as Boschendal and Groot Paardevlei, as well as in the San rock art paintings throughout the country.

The Arts and Crafts Movement (1870–1900) in Britain and the United States used stencils extensively and many of the William Morris fabric and wallpaper designs had their roots in stencils.

Famous artists used stencilling techniques, such as Pablo Picasso's designs for the *Ballet RuPablo* in the 1920s. Roy Lichtenstein, the renowned American artist, used stencilling over sheets of perforated metal to produce his comic-book-type art works.

By studying stencils made from vegetable fibres and animals skins, through paper and manila card, and finally to polyester film and Mylar™, it's possible to trace the development of stencils in tandem with the development of man. Today's stencils are cut with the aid of computers and laser technology – pity the poor Yoruban hammering out a stencil from roof sheeting with his chisel! Stencils are now available in thousands of designs, from hundreds of designers, and are obtainable throughout the world via craft shops and the Internet.

This book covers everything you need to know about making and painting your own stencils, including tips and shortcuts I have learned through trial and error. If you find that the stencil cutting itself is too difficult, all the designs featured in the projects are available, ready cut, from Outline Stencils (see the supplier list on page 127).

Stencilling remains the simplest, quickest and least expensive method of printing onto various surfaces, and over the years I have experimented with many techniques, with varying degrees of success. Here you will find the more successful ones and I hope you will be inspired to decorate your surroundings by means of this ancient art.

TOOLS AND MATERIALS

When I first started stencilling, there were no dedicated supplies available in South Africa so I had to make do with what I could find. To a certain extent, I still use these methods today. Although much of the following may sound technical and complicated, I have given simple, inexpensive alternatives for all the equipment that is required.

BRUSHES

When you stencil, apply the paint vertically in a swift pouncing or dabbing motion onto the surface to be decorated. Your brushes will take a hammering – literally and figuratively – so look after them. Brushes used for stencilling are always round, with short, stiff bristles and short handles to facilitate a dabbing motion, and to work the paint into the surface.

If you only intend completing a few projects, any round, inexpensive, artist's brush available from art or stationery shops may be used. Cut off the bristles short and level – about 1.5 cm from the steel binding – and then saw off the handle to a total length of 15 cm. Because the pig hair that the brush is made of will be damaged when the bristles are cut, the hair will 'split', and the brush will deteriorate fairly quickly, but you should have about two months' use out of the brush.

Proper stencil brushes are quite expensive, but with proper care will last for years. Look for a densely packed head of bristles that is firm, yet has a bit of 'give' when you bounce it on your hand. I also prefer bristles that are not too long.

You will need a brush for each colour you are using – I like to keep a few in reserve as well, as I find the brushes tend to soften while you are using them because they absorb the paint. You can wind a rubber band or wrap masking tape around the bristles to keep them stiff, but remove these before cleaning.

Use brushes that are in proportion to the open areas of the stencil – larger brushes for large areas and smaller ones for small spaces. Generally, I find that the brushes sold for stencilling are too large for convenience and I prefer to use a selection of brushes with heads 5–15 mm in diameter. However, this is a personal choice and you will have to experiment to find the brush size with which you are most comfortable. In the projects, I have specified the size of stencil brush that would be best to use and have graded them small, medium and large. The diameters are 5 mm, 10 mm and 15 mm, respectively.

Brushes should be cleaned immediately you have finished work for the day, either with warm water and a little dishwashing detergent for water-based paints, or with turpentine for oil-based products. Remove any rubber bands or masking tape if you have taped the bristles, before working the cleaning agent into the brush head and rinsing well. Store brushes with bristles uppermost until dry.

SPONGES

Small stencilling sponges can be made using an 8-cm square of 5-mm thick sponge formed into a firm ball around a wad of cottonwool or sponge and secured at the open end with a rubber band. (Larger sponges for use on floors can also be made in this manner – simply cut a larger square of foam.)

These little sponges work beautifully, giving a fine air-brushed look to the stencilling; the drawback is that they take a lot of time and your fingers will be covered in paint. However, they cost almost nothing and are disposable. They are also ideal for use with bronzing powders and paint glazes.

Miniature sponge paint rollers can be bought at any paint or hardware shop and are usually sold together with a paint tray. They are useful for covering large areas of a single colour but be careful to work the paint well into the roller before applying. Unfortunately, this method does use a lot more paint.

CUTTING KNIVES

Stencil cutting is a most precise task – both laborious and time consuming – therefore, a sharp knife that fits comfortably in the hand is almost essential. For one-off stencil cutting, cheap, plastic box cutters available from any hardware shop will do the trick, but if you are planning to do a lot of cutting, invest in a proper craft knife or paper scalpel and you will reap the benefits for years.

Look for a knife with a slim, pencil shape that fits comfortably in your hand, a textured handle and blades that can be replaced. Stationery, art and craft shops will stock these. My personal preference is an NT Cutter, size BD-400. The replaceable blades for these knives may be bought separately in packs of 100. After 20 years of stencil cutting, I still use my original knife and am on my sixth pack of blades!

Swivel knives have blades that move and are often recommended, but I must admit I have never tried one and am happy with my own.

ELECTRIC HEAT CUTTING TOOLS

When I first saw electric heat cutting tools advertised in an overseas magazine, I thought my prayers had been answered: an electric pen that looked like a soldering iron, which would simply melt the stencil as I traced the outline.

What a disappointment when, after much effort and expense, I finally obtained one – the heat pen certainly melted the plastic stencil material, but it left such an awful mess of melted plastic that it took me hours to scrape it all off. Worst of all, I discovered that I could not achieve a smooth cut and the electric cord was a nuisance as it constantly got in the way. The little, replaceable cutting nibs also bent after a short time and were not really fine enough so, for me, it was back to the knife.

CUTTING BOARDS

You need to protect your cutting surfaces otherwise you will end up with an irreparably damaged table top.

I first started cutting on pieces of corrugated board sourced from ordinary packing boxes, which is perfectly adequate for beginners, but will blunt your blades quite quickly.

Self-healing PVC cutting mats, available from stationery and art shops, are ideal as they lie flat, allow for a smooth cut and have a useful network of lines and squares on the surface. The dark green of the mats also shows up the stencil as you cut and you can make any necessary adjustments as you progress. One word of caution: DO NOT LEAVE THE MATS IN THE SUN or expose them to heat as they become hard and perish, and are then useless as a cutting surface. Unfortunately, the manufacturers do not specify this and are unwilling to replace them when this occurs.

ADHESIVES

Over the years I have come across many different ways of securing the stencil to the surface to be painted, but there is only one that I advise – an adhesive spray. It works 100% of the time and is totally reliable.

The adhesive spray or 'glue in a can' creates a tacky surface on the back of the stencil that allows repositioning at will. It holds the stencil in close contact with the surface you wish to decorate and prevents the paint from 'bleeding' under the edges and thus blurring the result.

These adhesives MUST be used in a well-ventilated area. Do not inhale the fumes and do not smoke while using the adhesives. It is not necessary to re-apply the adhesive every time you use the stencil, as it will remain sticky enough for a number of uses. Position the stencil upside down on newspaper before lightly spraying the stencil from about 30 cm away. Wait a few minutes before using.

This method can be used for all surfaces except ceramic bisqueware, although if you are using very large stencils for wall murals you will need to use masking tape as well to help hold the weight of the stencil.

Do be careful where you spray as you can leave a nasty, sticky film over floors and tables, and apply the spray with a light touch.

There are a number of different sprays on the market but ask your craft shop for advice on one in which the spray nozzle is unlikely to clog or cause irritation. In the event of the nozzle clogging, try a short spray with the can upside down and, if this does not clear the blockage, it may be necessary to clean the nozzle with some thinners or adhesive remover.

If you use adhesive spray, your stencils will be sticky, so store them in plastic bags, A4 file folders or dust them lightly with baby powder to remove the stickiness.

Other methods of securing stencils that I have encountered include small pieces of adhesive putty, masking tape, inserting lots of little pins or an awful sticky paste that you paint on the back of the stencil – not recommended!

SHIELDS

Shields are small pieces of leftover PVC or stencil material that have various curves and shapes cut into them. They are extremely useful in keeping colours from overlapping, adding veins to leaves and shading shapes into areas. I keep a supply of them handy when working and clean them with the stencils.

PAINTS

The extensive range of paints available is impossible to list here. Follow one rule: try it, if it works – use it!

Be adventurous and experiment with different paints on various surfaces. I have included results that I have found to be successful. Many different types of paint have been used in the projects in this book to give you an idea of the endless range of possibilities.

Basically, all paints are pigments (colours) mixed into a carrying medium that can either be oil- or water-based. As we know, oil and water do not mix or, that is, not until recently as I discovered when I tried an oil-based paint cream and was able to clean the brushes in detergent and water.

As a general rule, water-based paints are much easier to work with because they are simple to clean up, although the rich, creaminess of the oil paints and the intensity of colour they carry are sometimes worth the extra effort required. Stencilling is very economical with paint and only a tiny amount is necessary to cover a large area.

FABRIC PAINT

There have been some exciting recent innovations in the fabric paint industry. These paints are widely available with many small craft outlets producing their own ranges of paints.

The pigments are mixed into a water-based, porridge-like emulsion that is also sold separately – either as an extender to stretch the paint or as a base to mix your own colours. When I first started stencilling, these inks were only sold by the silkscreen industry and individual colours had to be bought by the kilogram. As you can imagine, it took years to use them up!

To judge if a fabric paint is suitable for stencilling, hold the container upside-down and if the contents all rush towards the lid, the paint is far too thin and will not give good results; you need a paint the consistency of smooth peanut butter to prevent bleeding and seepage under the stencil.

Normal fabric paints are transparent and will only cover a light-coloured surface, so opaque or semi-opaque paints are required for darker fabrics. These paints are generally much thicker and denser as they need to cover the fabric thoroughly.

In addition to the large range of colours available, there are also pearlised, metallic and puff paints suitable for use in fabric stencilling. Most of these fabric paints require curing by the application of heat in order to make them washable. There are, however, new paints available that do not need heat-curing.

FABRIC LINERS

Liners are basically fabric paints in a bottle with a nib-like lid and are useful for adding detail. They are available in glitters, 3D (which dry raised, creating little beads of colour), pearlised and metallic effects.

OIL-BASED FABRIC PAINT

Also suitable for use on fabrics are the oil-based, solid, paint creams sold in little tubs, much like lip gloss. They have the consistency of lipstick and form a skin on the surface of the paint that must be removed each time they are used. A firm wipe with a paper towel is normally enough to expose the usable paint, but do be careful with the discarded skins as they tend to migrate everywhere and a small spot dropped mistakenly on a carpet can grow to epic proportions and be extremely difficult to remove.

Paint creams create a lovely rich, intense colour and shade beautifully. The metallics in this range are especially good, for instance golds that are subtle rather than glittery. The creams are all imported and therefore quite expensive but they do last for ages. They work well on pile fabrics such as velvet and velour and sheers such as voile and organza. Paint creams do not need heat-curing but do take up to two weeks to cure before they are rendered washable. Brushes can be cleaned in warm water and detergent.

I have used fabric paints on exterior and interior walls covered in water-based paint, on wooden floors, cement floors, cement asbestos flower pots, towelling and cotton rugs as well as many different fabric types and have found them to be excellent and extremely versatile. They take a little longer than PVA to dry when applied to walls, thus giving you time to mix and blend the colours for a lovely shaded effect.

SPRAY PAINT

Available in a wide variety of fade-free colours, spray paints are an exciting medium to use and are unrivalled for the delicate, airy results they produce. They include metallics, which give a soft sheen if used discreetly, and textured paints, which create a hammered-metal finish or sandstone effect. I love the way the spray touches the surface resulting in a subtle blending of one area into another, as when the green of a leaf has just a hint of the red flower next to it.

Aerosol paints dry very quickly – they are drying as the paint leaves the can – so you do not have to wait to move your stencil for repeats. Stencilling with aerosol spray paints is quite different to other types of stencilling. There is no close contact with the stencil itself and great care must be taken to mask off all areas surrounding the stencil so that none of the drift from the spray falls onto your surface as it is well nigh impossible to remove. The stencil is prepared and secured to the surface in the usual manner, using an adhesive spray. Fix newsprint in a frame around the stencil border with masking tape. Tape the paper down because if it is only laid on top of the stencil, some of the paint may still find its way underneath.

Aerosol paints should be shaken very firmly for at least a minute to agitate the paint and mix it well. The tins all have a little marble inside for mixing purposes and you can hear it rattling around when shaken. Take care to use these paints only in a well-ventilated space as they contain solvents to keep the paint liquid; inhaling this for an extended period of time will leave you feeling lightheaded and with a bad headache. If you are pregnant, avoid the use of aerosol paints altogether. Do not eat or drink while working with aerosol paints and, of course, avoid smoking.

Hold the can approximately 15–20 cm away from the surface you are stencilling. Practise first until you are comfortable with the distance, the nozzle direction and the amount of paint that is released. Try to avoid a burst of paint building up in one place – this happens when the nozzle is held too close to the surface or depressed for too long. If you find the paint running or appearing liquid on the stencil, you are spraying too much paint.

A gentle pumping action on the nozzle will give soft bursts of spray and you should aim for this, rather than a long, solid release of colour. The nozzle will feel a little stiff at first but it becomes easier to depress with use. To achieve the correct action, imagine you are pressing an egg and are scared of breaking it. It requires quite a bit of pressure to depress the nozzle and your fingers will tire quite quickly, so rest them frequently.

Allow the stencil to dry thoroughly in between each application – this will only take about two minutes and will prevent you from smearing paint on your hands and spreading it around to other surfaces. If you hold a piece of cardboard in front of the stencil and direct the bursts of spray onto it, the drift from the paint will fall onto the stencil giving a lovely, delicate result. Bits of cardboard can be folded and used to direct the spray or to shield areas of the stencil.

For small areas, cut a hole in a piece of cardboard a little bigger than the area you wish to stencil and place this over the section in your stencil. Direct the nozzle to apply paint to only that section. Do not over apply the paint – even the lightest application appears quite vivid once the stencil is removed. It is always possible to add more paint but very difficult to remove it.

An annoying problem with spray paints is clogged nozzles; a short burst sprayed outside with the can upside down should clear the opening. Alternatively, you may have to remove the nozzle and soak it in nail varnish remover or thinners to clear the blockage. Use the ozone-friendly types of aerosol sprays – they are usually marked CFC-free.

BRONZING POWDERS

Strictly speaking not a paint, bronzing powders are also sold under the name pigment powders. For more information, see page 33

PAINTS FOR CERAMICS

Paints suitable for stencilling onto bisqueware are obtainable from pottery supply shops. They are tricky to work with in that the colour of the paint is not necessarily the colour of the final result once the article has been fired in a kiln.

Most pottery supplies shops stock samples of the colours once they have been fired, to give you a better idea of the end result. There are paints available that may be painted directly onto glazed and fired pottery but I have found them to be unsuitable for stencilling. The latest tile primers do, however, allow one to paint onto fired tiles or other smooth, non-absorbent surfaces.

PVA

Polyvinyl acrylics (PVAs) are the normal type of wall paints. They are suitable for stencilling on walls and I usually use them with fabric paints. Drawbacks are that they dry very quickly and are only obtainable in one-litre containers. A few years ago, the paint companies produced tiny sample pots of PVA in a limited range of colours and these were fantastic for stencillers but unfortunately these have been discontinued. A solution is to ask family or friends for small quantities of leftover paint standing around in their sheds and garages.

PAINTS TO BE AVOIDED

Paints that I have not had a great deal of success with include: craft paints – they dry too quickly and leave an awful, lumpy mess on the brushes; oil-based enamel paints and on-glaze ceramic paints are very messy, run everywhere and are impossible to clean off the stencil; and oil-based paint in crayons require just too much muscular effort and are very expensive.

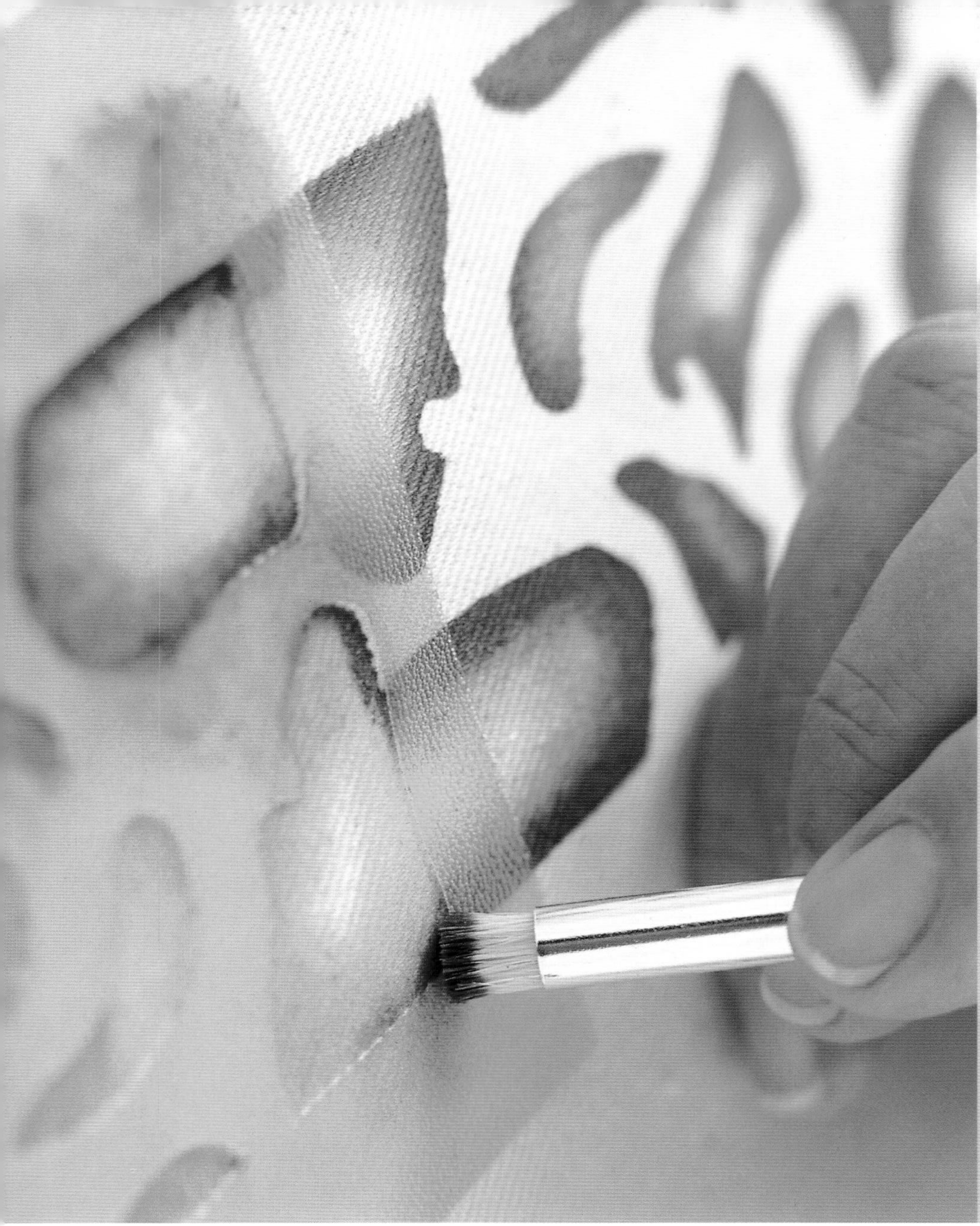

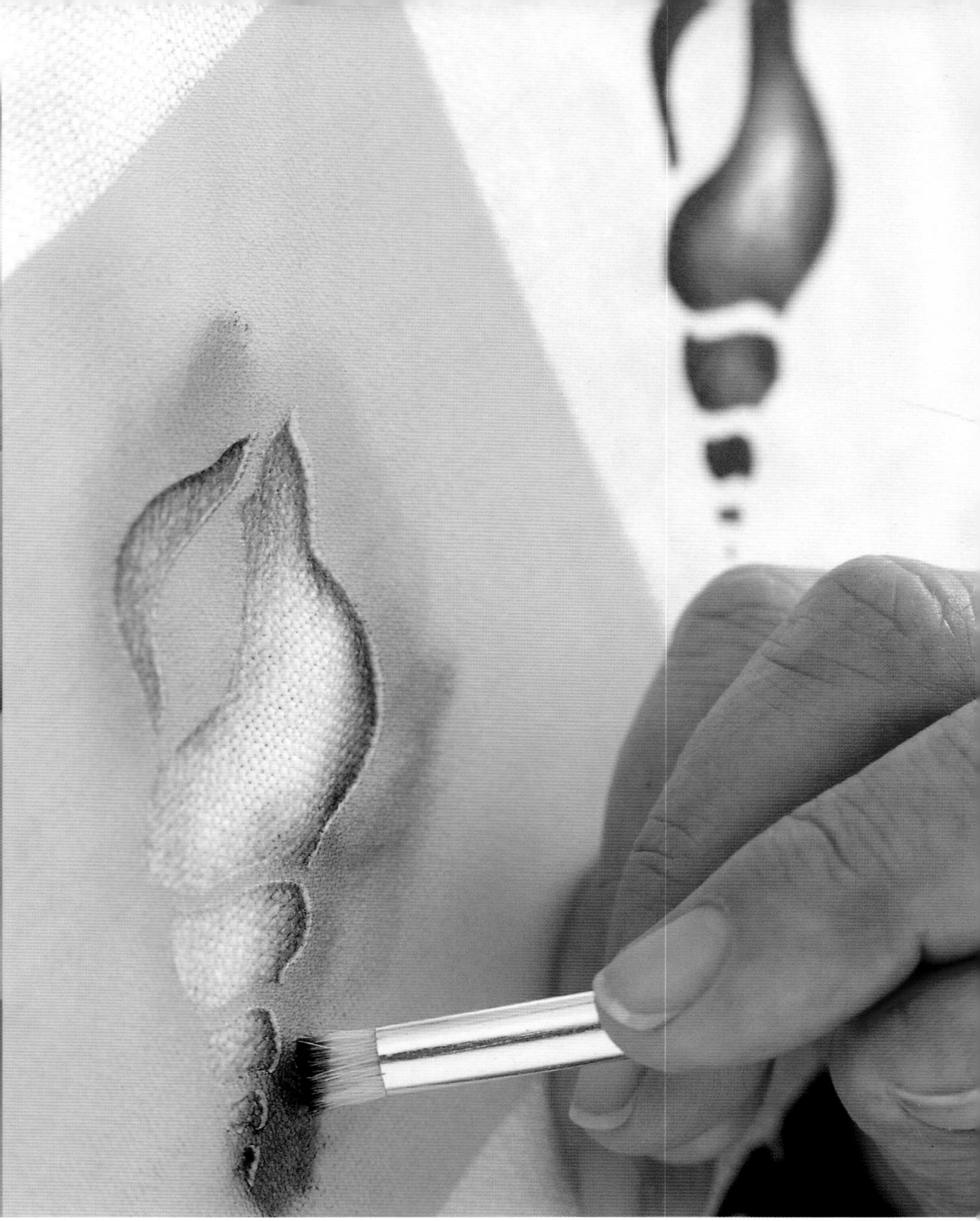

STENCILS

STENCIL DESIGNING

In very basic terms, a stencil is a sheet of material with holes or windows cut into it and through which paint is applied to print an image. Although there are a myriad ready-cut stencils available, you might want to design your own to match with curtains, to customise a room or simply to create an idea of your own. You do not need to be an artist to design a stencil – there are thousands of images that could be used as a basis for a design. Once you are accustomed to looking for stencilled images, you will notice them everywhere – in the classified columns of magazines, in advertisements, painted on trucks you pass on the road, even the road signs themselves. Stencils are a part of our everyday lives and always have been.

A very simple motif may be repeated and linked with a simple curve to create a border. The outline of a leaf forms a simple but effective stencil or it could be broken up into smaller areas to define veins and stem.

The stencilling process itself will transform the completed image into a pleasing, artistic result. A successful stencil has rhythm and movement in its design, rather than a static, stiff look.

The little pieces that link the different areas of the design are called 'bridges'. These play two important roles in the stencil – they hold the design together and lend strength to the stencil itself. In a successful stencil design, the bridges form an integral part of the image,

for example, the bridge that shows the curve of a bird's wing defines the feathers on the wing or separates the bird's eye from the rest of the face, according to the markings of that particular species.

Depending on the species, bridges can be used to define the characteristics of the bird or animal involved. Here a bridge has been cut around the eye area.

Bridges should be of a uniform size throughout the stencil and also be in proportion to the size of the stencil; a small stencil will have delicate bridges while a large mural stencil will have more robust bridges. Do not make the bridges so narrow that they break easily – the Japanese used bridges the width of a human hair for their stencils, but you need not go that far!

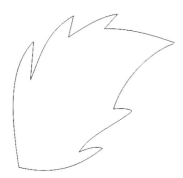

In the first leaf illustrated above, a simple outline stencil is used. The second shows how a bridge can be used to define the vein, while the third leaf is cut as a two-part stencil, with the vein detail added to the outline.

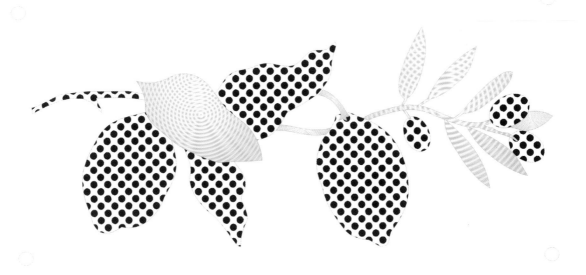

When designing a two-layered stencil, areas that adjoin must be cut separately as they share a common border. In the illustration above, all the areas shaded with dots are cut on one stencil and the grey areas are cut on a second stencil. Note the position of the registration holes, which must be cut on both stencils.

If you want a multi-layered stencil, the bridges fall away as the completed design will create a total, hand-painted effect. In order to make these stencils, each adjoining area of the design must be numbered so that areas that share a common border do not have the same numbers. You may end up with three or four different stencils that need to be cut. Mark a registration point at each of the four corners of your design; these are essential for matching up your design once you come to stencilling it. Once the areas have been numbered (remember you are separating areas not different colours), the required number of copies of the design need to be made. If you have numbered four different areas, make four photocopies. This will be covered in more detail later.

Also bear in mind the area for which you are designing the stencil; if you need a stencil for a small bathroom, a border with a width of 10 cm will look better than a heavier border of 15 cm. You'll be surprised how a simple stencil border can change the entire look of a room and visually alter its proportions.

Photocopying machines are invaluable when it comes to reducing or enlarging a design. You can even make reasonable photocopies from fabric and tiles, but be aware of the copyright that exists on various designs. There are plenty of copyright-free images available – gift wrap paper, for example, carries no copyrights and there are many copyright-free design books available.

The designs in this book may be used for your own personal use but may not be cut for sale.

CUTTING THE STENCIL

Various types of materials may be used for your stencils. Do you remember the boxed stencil kits with yellow Manila paper stencils that were available for children? Manila card, treated with linseed oil, may still be used, but I have used acetate (275 µ) for many years and find this to be most satisfactory. It is cheap, readily available at most art and craft shops, and is often sold by the metre.

Its advantages include:

- It is transparent, so you can attach the acetate to the print of the design and cut on the reverse side.
- It is easy to position the stencil on the surface to be printed because you can see through it and therefore place border repeats correctly.
- It is extremely tough and hardwearing – the edges of the design never 'feather' or wear, yet it is flexible enough to allow close contact with the surface to be printed.

A possible drawback to acetate is that it is very smooth and a little tricky for a beginner to cut. An alternative is PVC with a textured side – to give the cutting knife something to grip. It is available from most stationery shops in various colours, often sold as 'file covers'.

Use masking tape or adhesive putty to affix the design to the acetate (including all corners and sides) so that the design does not move while you are cutting.

For stencils that are only intended to be used once or twice, a firm card or paper is suitable, but a copy of the design will either have to be drawn onto the surface of the paper, or a photocopy fixed to the surface. Thereafter, the stencil must be cut through both layers of paper.

Some photocopy shops will copy directly onto a card (a weight of 60 g will be sufficient) so that you can cut your stencil directly from the card.

Thin paper stencils are used for stencilling onto unfired ceramic ware, but as these are dampened, they may only be used once. Newspaper or normal copier paper is suitable for this and it is possible to cut more than one stencil at a time if you layer the paper. When cutting paper stencils, a very sharp blade is required to achieve a good, clean edge.

Either cut on a self-healing cutting board – an excellent investment if you plan to do a lot of cutting as

An example of the cutting of a multi-layered stencil. Note the numbered areas; here all the number '1' areas are being cut.

the dark green of the board shows up any areas of jagged cutting while the white lines are useful guidelines – or on a piece of corrugated cardboard. It is essential to place some kind of protective material underneath when you cut; do not underestimate the depth of the cutting knife as you will end up with a heavily scored table surface.

Hold the knife at a slight angle to the acetate, as this will give you a clean, bevelled edge. Start cutting the design from the centre, cutting the smaller areas before the larger ones because the more you cut into your material, the weaker it becomes and you run the risk of putting too much pressure on the stencil and breaking the bridges. Always cut towards yourself, bearing in mind that you are using a razor-sharp blade so keep 'extra' fingers out of the way. This may sound obvious but it is easy to become so engrossed in what you are doing that slip-ups occur.

With multi-layered stencils, make sure that you cut on the outer edge of the design's lines so that the areas will join up when printing. It might not seem like much but that additional bit ensures smooth joins without gaps. Cut curves in one, smooth stroke, turning the stencil rather than attempting to move your arm around the corners. A common problem for beginners is rough, jagged edges on curves; these will print as they are cut, with not very pleasing results.

The little bits you cut out should almost pop out of the stencil as you cut, or should come free with a little pressure. A wastepaper bin is useful to keep nearby for the bits. Mistakes and cut bridges can be easily fixed by applying a little adhesive tape to both sides of the stencil and recutting the area. You may join two pieces of stencil material in a similar manner. If you find that your arm and shoulders start to ache, you are applying far too much pressure – relax and cut from the wrist.

If the stencil bridges break, apply adhesive tape to both sides of the stencil and recut.

LETTERING AND NUMBERS

A useful and practical stencilling application is to create lettering for projects and, with access to a computer, it is easy to find many interesting styles of writing. It may be that a sports team needs T-shirts printed with team numbers and names, a business needs overalls with its company name for workers, or that you want to produce clothing with witty sayings or tourist articles with their origin on them. Even birthday cards can be printed and embossed with professional results.

In addition, lettering can provide an interesting and welcome alternative to ornamental designs. A functional article boldly stencilled with its use can be very stylish, for example an umbrella with 'Rain' emblazoned on it. Inexpensive muslin or calico can be stencilled with 'Gift' and used to wrap a present in an unusual way. With the easy accessibility to hundreds of different fonts and writing styles on home computers,

and their ability to alter size and shape easily, it makes the entire process that much simpler.

Bear in mind that, unless you cut layered stencils, you will have to cut bridges in any letter with a closed loop in it, for instance 'o', 'e', 'b'. The normal Stencil font is a standard font on most computers and is, of course, the easiest to use as the letters are already bridged, but it is not always suitable or the correct style for a particular project. Many other fonts also have bridges, such as Futura Black, while some lend themselves more easily to adaptation, such as Forte, Papyrus and Poor Richard.

As with all stencil cutting, the smaller the area to cut, the more difficult it becomes. In my experience lettering cut to a height of 1.5 cm is the lower limit.

To cut a layered lettering stencil, the same concept is used as for all multi-layered stencils. Make two copies of the required lettering, not forgetting to mark four registration points and number the front of each stencil.

Printing of a lettering stencil in two parts: the second print completes the letters with closed loops.

Letters such as 'a', 'b', 'e', and 'o' with an enclosed loop, as well as any decorative loops, must be cut in two sections. Try cutting the stem of the letter on one stencil and the loop on the other. 'O's are best cut with half on each stencil.

To print, simply lay the first sprayed stencil down, mark your four registration points and print. Remove and lay the second stencil down over the registration marks and print. Remove and *voilá!*, you have perfect lettering any screen printer would be proud to claim.

PRINTING A STENCIL

The best part of the entire process is printing the stencil you have just spent hours cutting out for the first time. Once you have decided on your colours, paints and surface, you are ready to begin.

Lightly spritz the back of your stencil with the adhesive spray, wait a few minutes for it to dry and secure it to your printing surface. If you think the stencil is too sticky, press it onto a T-shirt or similar fabric to pick up a little of the fluff and reduce the stickiness.

Transfer a little of the paint to the container lid with a dry stencil brush and work from the lid, replenishing as needed. Never dip your brush into the paint container and work from there as you will have far too much paint on your brush and it will mess and run under the stencil. Do not dilute the paint, as it will become too thin.

A golden rule while stencilling is to use as little paint as possible and build up the intensity of colour with many light applications rather than one heavy layer. Too much paint makes the final effect heavy and crude; your goal should be a light, lively effect. With a light, quick, dabbing motion, apply the paint onto your surface, working at a slight angle from the edges of the stencil – this will secure the stencil more firmly to the surface and give definition to the end result. Ignore any small bits of paint drifting onto neighbouring areas – they will add to the final effect and not be seen as an error. To separate colours, use a shield to protect adjoining areas.

Hold the stencil brush firmly at a slight angle and apply the paint with a quick, dabbing motion.

By using gradually darker shades of the same colour in ever-widening areas, it is possible to create a 3D-like effect and give life to the stencil. Leaving areas of light in the middle adds to this illusion, while using a different colour as a base to an area can highlight it and almost makes it glow.

Once the stencil print is completed, carefully peel away the stencil by gently loosening any delicate bridges, then sit back and admire your work!

CLEANING THE STENCIL

Unless paint has seeped under your stencil, it is unnecessary to wash it between printings – simply lie it paint side down onto newspaper to absorb any excess paint. When the project is completed, the stencil can be cleaned by soaking it in warm water and a little dishwashing detergent. Keep an old nailbrush handy for scrubbing the stencil, but be careful not to catch and tear the little bridges. Fabric paint can be removed very easily; after a short soak in warm water the paint loosens and is easy to scrape off. PVA dries quickly and, if left on the stencil too long, is nearly impossible to clean off, so wash it as soon as possible.

A build-up of adhesive spray may be removed with turpentine and a scraper, but is a messy job so do this on lots of newspaper. This is really only necessary if the tiny windows on a stencil become clogged by adhesive. It is not necessary to buy expensive adhesive remover.

MISTAKES

Mistakes and accidents are bound to occur and sometimes efforts to fix them only make them worse. Most mistakes are caused by dirty fingers, dropping the brushes or even knocking over the paint container. To avoid any of these from happening, use a cardboard box to hold all the paints and lids you are using and keep a damp rag handy for wiping fingers and hands. If you are working on a wall or other hard surface, have a little of the background colour ready to cover any errors if a damp ear bud does not clear the mistake.

Mistakes on fabric are more difficult to fix, as the surface is so absorbent. Try to avoid errors and be extra careful. On fabric a light mark can be removed by gently rubbing the area with a damp sponge before you set the paint. Do not use bleach as this will discolour the whole area and make it even more obvious. Bigger, darker splotches could be covered with a small stencil of something appropriate, e.g. a small bee, butterfly or spiral. Many a large tablecloth I have printed has been saved by the strategic placement of an insect!

Check the back of the stencil for paint smudges each time before repositioning it. Remove these immediately or they will be transferred with every printing.

STORAGE AND REPAIR OF STENCILS

Stencils must be stored flat – I keep my smaller ones in a file in separate plastic sleeves and the larger stencils in a large, plastic portfolio-sized flip file. Use a separate sleeve for each stencil or you will end up with a sticky sandwich of stencils that will tear when you try to pry them apart.

Stencil bridges may be torn either by catching on something or in the washing process. Broken stencils are easily repaired but first try to make a copy of the stencil before cutting away the loose piece. Stick masking tape on either side of the broken area and recut that section. The tape will come off after washing a few times but is easy enough to replace.

If you do not have a sheet of stencil material large enough for the design you want to cut, make a neat join by ensuring that the edges you wish to join are perfectly straight, butt them together and tape with masking tape on both sides of the stencil material. Cuts can then be made right across the join without any ill effects.

COLOUR
WHEEL

COLOUR

Although colour choice is a matter of personal taste and fashion, this chapter is intended only as a guide to those less confident in choosing colours. It demonstrates the colour and shade blending that give stencilling its impact.

The easiest way to understand colours and their composition is to remember that the primary colours are red, blue and yellow. Every other colour is made from these three plus black and white. Primary colours generally appeal to the young. On a colour wheel, these colours are positioned as three compass points and the colour directions in between them are the hues.

Secondary colours are a mixture of two of the three primary colours and are found halfway between tose two primary colours. Two colours directly across from each other on the wheel are contrasting colours, while colours next to each other are complementary or harmonious. Any colour mixed with white becomes a tint and colours with black added are shades. Colours that have black and white added are tones and are always more subtle than the original colour – these are the ones that I use the most. Neutrals or non-colours such as browns, creams and greys are not to be forgotten and are particularly useful when combined with textured effects.

You may find it helpful to look at the paint sample displays in a hardware shop. These are arranged in differing shades and tones of the same colour and are an excellent way of judging how the colours look next to each other. Booklets and leaflets supplied by the paint companies are also mines of inspiration and they are free! The only problem is that the range of colours is so large that it is difficult to stay focused. It is best to have a very definite idea of what you want to achieve so that you are not sidetracked by the choice.

It is not always necessary to opt for contrast when stencilling a motif or border. A colour that is just a shade or two lighter or darker than the base surface looks more classy and sophisticated. The new 'chalky', matt colours are lovely and, together with the huge selection of neutral and natural tones, result in a much gentler finish.

Over the years, I have found that the more subtle tones of colour are infinitely more successful than bold, brash ones, and that two or more shades of the same colour, applied in layers and blended, create a far more natural, and therefore pleasing, effect than one definite application. Complementary colours applied one over the other, from lightest to darkest, also result in an almost glowing, rounded look. Take leaves as an example: the more time and effort I spend on stencilling the leaves in a design, the better the overall look. I normally start with a layer of a yellow (a light, lemon yellow is best), after which I apply at least two shades of green in ever-increasing circles, so that the centre of each leaf is lighter and the outer edges are lined with a darker shade.

A simple addition of the leaf vein in the same colour as the darkest green used, with the aid of a plastic shield, has a magical effect.

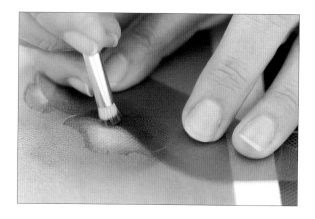

Stay away from the bright apple greens and instead use sludgy olives, khakis and bottle greens. If possible, look at the actual leaf in nature before you start, as rose leaves differ totally from oak, and olive leaves are a wonderful silvery-grey colour. Cerise pink applied under violet makes an effective combination for flowers such as fuchsias and roses.

For yellow flowers or fruit, try starting with the lightest shade of yellow (such as lemon), then apply a sunny yellow lightly over it and edge the area with a hint of orange. Your design will come to life immediately. A subtle touch of olive green to one side of fruit also gives a more natural look.

If you are stencilling red fruit such as strawberries or cherries, print a base colour of scarlet red leaving a very definite white area in the centre and edge with maroon or burgundy.

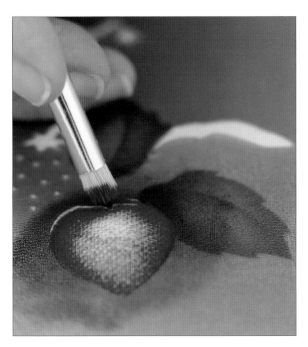

Grapes look best with the berries in a combination of burgundy edged with plum or violet.

An invaluable tip in creating animals or rock art stencils is to first cover the whole area with a sunny yellow. Lightly apply terracotta over the top, leaving the central areas light enough to see the yellow, then edge with a dark chocolate brown. This works well for giraffe and buck designs.

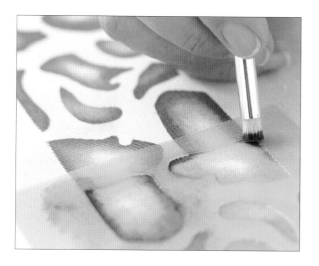

A touch of gold at the edges of the dark brown works wonders on rock art motifs. In fact, I have found that a little gold paint applied over almost any colour, ages and softens it.

Black and gold, or brown and gold, create really beautiful African borders and what could look entirely wrong in a Eurocentric design, somehow looks just right with these simple geometric shapes.

Blues, greens and lilacs are excellent combinations when creating a beach or marine stencil colour scheme. A layer of French blue over an apple green is wonderful for an instant nautical or 'sea feel'.

Blues and greens, when edged with a hint of violet, are reminiscent of periwinkles and breaking waves.

For a really sophisticated effect, a cream-on-cream combination is best. The cream may either be in the form of a textured paint, or as an opaque paint on a sheer background.

Naturally, these are only my suggestions and you will discover your own favourite colours and combinations as you work with them and learn what works for you.

STENCILLING ON FABRIC

Stencilling on fabric works extremely well and if the fabric paint is correctly cured, the article will be completely washable.

In my experience, the best results are usually obtained by using a natural fabric such as cotton, linen or canvas (sold as PFP), which has been prepared for printing. In effect, this means that it has no finish that could affect the absorption of the fabric paint into the fabric.

Any fabric that contains man-made fibres tends to repel the fabric paint and also causes it to bleed along these fibres. Although synthetic blends may be used, as a precaution I would limit their use to articles that do not need much washing, or by using spray paints in place of fabric paints.

A general test to see if fabric is suitable for fabric paint is to drop a little water onto the surface; if it is immediately absorbed, it should take the fabric paint, but if the water forms a little bubble on the surface, it is best not to use it as the fabric will not absorb the paint well enough to be washable.

Cotton muslin prints well and is suitable for articles such as filmy, airy curtains and beach sarongs. Remember to work on sheets of absorbent paper, as the fabric paint will seep right through the open weave of the fabric. Heavy canvas called 'cotton duck', because of its ability to shed water, may be used for deck chairs and floor cloths, and also absorbs fabric paint very well, but should be protected before use. Deckchair covers may be Scotchguarded™ and the floor cloths varnished.

Indian cotton dhurries in plain colours are suitable items on which to stencil, but require quite vigorous stencilling to push the paint into the heavily textured surface. I have not had very good results using calico and therefore prefer to use hopsack linen for tablecloths and cushion covers.

Bull denim is suitable where a heavier fabric is needed e.g. shopping bags, oven gloves and laundry bags. Stencilling onto blue denim with light colours requires a base coat of white opaque fabric paint before using lighter colours on top.

T-shirts print extremely well and wash well too, but make sure they are 100% cotton and do not forget to insert a piece of cardboard or plastic to prevent the paint seeping straight through to the other side!

Cotton towelling also prints well but, unfortunately, absorbs a lot more paint. Pretty details may be added to facecloths and towels, but for the best result make sure that the pile is all lying in one direction before you start printing.

It's important to keep in mind that the texture of a fabric adds to the overall finish of the stencilled article – the smoother the fabric, the finer the result, while rougher fabrics add interest to ethnic and animal prints. Bolton cloth (previously known as heavy or K-sheeting) is also suitable for an ethnic look. The background colour of a fabric can play an important role in the final result, so choose a colour that will complement the design you are stencilling.

An enormous, blank area of fabric, for example a tablecloth or a duvet cover, can be quite daunting. I usually iron the fabric into squares before beginning a project and then use the ironed lines as a grid guide to plan the position of the design. It is generally easier to stencil an article before it is made up, but in the case of tablecloths it is best to complete the hems first in order to position the borders correctly.

Using an oil-based paint cream, synthetic fabrics such as organza and voile may be stencilled with beautiful, delicate results. Aerosol spray paints also work well on synthetics and are completely washable.

There are many different makes of fabric paint available. Until you have gained your own experience, your local craft store should be able to advise you on a brand that produces professional, reliable results, particularly as the consistency of the paint is so important in stencilling.

CURING FABRIC PAINTS

Before fabric paint is cured you can feel it on the surface of the fabric. Once cured, however, it becomes an integral part of the fabric. Most fabric paints need to be cured by the application of dry heat to render them washable. This can be done by:

- Placing the article into a clean oven set at 130 °C for 15 minutes with the painted side of the fabric folded to the inside. Switch off the oven with the item inside and leave to cool down, OR
- Placing it into a tumble dryer on a high setting for 45 minutes, OR
- Ironing the item with a dry iron on a cotton setting, starting with the reverse side and then the painted side.

Once this process is complete, the article may be machine-washed, on a regular cycle, at a recommended temperature of 45 °C. However, if in doubt, contact the manufacturers of the paint you are using for their specific recommendations.

RESIST STENCILLING

In the course of my research for this book, I came across some fascinating facts, such as the use by the Yoruba tribe in Nigeria of a form of stencilling that uses a starch-resist technique.

I have since discovered that this was used by many other cultures in different forms. Basically it is a form of resist-dyeing whereby a starch paste is applied through the stencil and allowed to dry. The article is then dipped in dye and when it has dried it is washed in warm water to remove the paste.

I use a similar technique, but with a bit of a twist. Instead of dying a light cloth, I use dark, bull denim and bleach to strip the colour from the fabric and reveal the stencilled design. The result is an earthy, African look that complements any simple, bold African designs. However, you will need to test the fabric first to see if it will react to the bleach, but this is easily done on a small corner of fabric using an ear bud dipped in ordinary household bleach.

Mix about two tablespoons of flour and three tablespoons water to form a thick but smooth paste – about the same consistency as a cake batter. The paste will become quite elastic and may be kept overnight in a closed container if necessary.

After first applying adhesive spray, position your stencil in the desired position. Using a cake spatula, spread a little of the paste over the stencil. Press the paste firmly into the fabric, then wipe off the excess with the spatula. Try to keep the paste level with the surface of the stencil.

Remove the stencil. If any of the paste has seeped onto the back of the stencil, wash and dry before continuing. You may find that where the paste is too thick it creates a rougher outline – don't worry too much because this will merely add to the character of the print. Once you have completed the starch-resist, leave it to dry. As the paste dries, it will pucker the fabric, but this is normal.

Using a paintbrush with a width of 5 cm, quickly paint bleach over the entire item. The fabric will start to lighten almost immediately. When the fabric has reached the desired shade, rinse under running water to stop the activation of the bleach. If you would like more control over the bleaching action, dilute the bleach with water, which will prevent it from working quite as fast. However, you may need to apply the solution more than once.

Soak the fabric in warm water, then scrape off the paste as it softens. The stencil will gradually be revealed as the paste comes away. You may need to hang the fabric on the washing line and hose it down to remove any remaining paste, which can be highly resistant to removal. If you wish, further details may be added to the design with fabric paint or liners once the fabric has dried completely.

STENCILLING WITH PUFF PAINT

Working with puff paints is great fun and adds a tactile dimension to your project. I first experimented with this on an animal paw print stencil and the little suede, raised paws were so appealing that I have used the paint with many other stencils. Puff paints are available in a range of colours but I particularly like the cream-on-cream effect I used on a cushion cover (see detail below).

A fairly heavy fabric is required to 'hold' the paint, which means that synthetics are completely unsuitable because you need a hot iron to create the puff. The best way to achieve a successful result is to use a dry iron (do not attempt it with a steam iron) on a cotton setting.

Wait until the iron has reached the appropriate temperature, then slowly press the iron once over the fabric on the wrong side. You will actually see the little indentations form as the iron passes over the paint. Do not be tempted to iron too much or the paint will puff up to such an extent that it bloats and peels off – you are aiming for a suede-like, slightly raised effect, not a puffy, distorted one.

The paint itself is applied as you would with any other type of stencilling. However, you do need quite a thick layer so this is one occasion when it's necessary to use quite a bit of paint.

Remember, only one layer is required, as there is no shading involved.

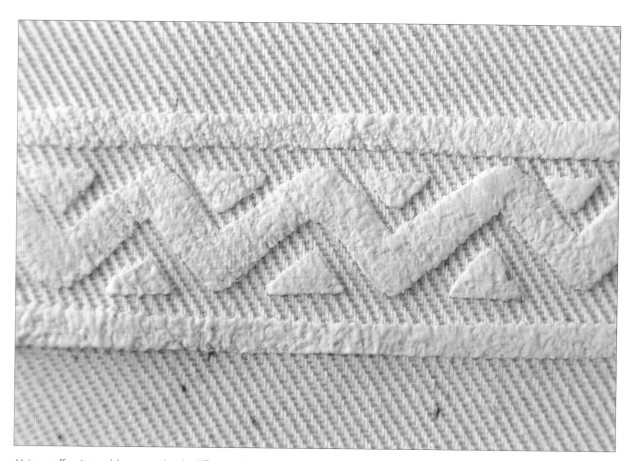

Using puff paints adds a completely different dimension to the texture of the fabric on which you're working. Here a cream-coloured puff paint has been applied to a rough bull denim to create a raised border that has a suede-like appearance. This could also be applied in a contrasting coloured puff paint depending on the desired effect.

MOSAIC STENCILLING

Mosaics have seen a meteoric rise in popularity in recent years and have become sought after, for both domestic and commercial interior decoration. They add a richness and style that remains unrivalled from ancient times, but the time and expertise required to create these works puts them beyond the reach of most of us. However, with a mosaic stencil, although initially time-consuming to cut and design, repeats are easy and quick to apply and the effect is just as magical.

The first time I saw a mosaic stencil, at a coffee shop in Hermanus (see opposite), I was completely enthralled at how a simple room could be transformed by a Grecian work of art. I managed to track down Tina Beaumont, who had completed this epic project as well as another breathtaking one in the sister coffee shop in Kleinmond. Tina studied textile design at the Cape Technikon and had done a lot of stencil cutting while there. She developed her ideas for the mosaics from pictures of ancient mosaics on the island of Cyprus. Her use of soft, chalky colours against a broken cream background and the way the stencil imitates a ruin contribute to the authentic result.

Cement floors can also be transformed into gorgeous works of art and are completely practical to keep clean – a simple wipe with a mop and spills and breakages will be harmless. Wooden tables and bathroom walls are also suitable surfaces for mosaic stencilling. But be warned – everyone who sees the finished projects will want them too!

Prior planning is essential to form a complete picture of what you want to achieve and is well worth the time and effort. Page through books on mosaics and look for pictures of ancient Greek and Roman architecture for design ideas. But remember to keep your design simple – a small border can be as effective as a complex one. The size of the design should also be in proportion to the area you wish to decorate.

Mosaic tiles or tesserae are usually manufactured in 15 x 15-mm squares, so bear this in mind when planning your design. I usually cut the 'tiles' slightly smaller – 10 x 10 mm – but this depends on the size of the area. Do not worry about getting the stencil tiles exactly square and straight when cutting, as a little irregularity adds authenticity to the final effect.

It is important to study how tiles are laid in actual mosaic designs – they have a flow, a movement called *andamento*, around the focal point of the design. They are often applied in a row around the central motif to emphasise the lines of the design, known as the *opus vermiculatum*. These Latin terms are not meant to scare you off, but to assist you so that you will recognise what they mean should you come across them in your design research.

Draw the central motif first and divide it into squares following the lines of the motif. In stairs (see page 85), I used a gecko morif and you will notice how the lines of the tiles emphasise the shape of the body. The area surrounding the motif may then be planned and the *opus vermiculatum* can be incorporated before completing the rest of the design.

Leave a generous border around the design when cutting so that no paint is accidentally spilled over the edges while working with the stencil. Clean the stencil immediately after use – you might need to clean it after a few repeats as the small, square holes become clogged quite quickly.

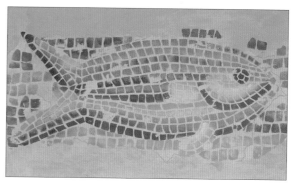

A fish detail of the mosaic stencil created by Tina Beaumont at the Europa coffee shop in Hermanus.

STENCILLING ON PAPER

There is absolutely no difficulty in stencilling on paper and really beautiful effects can be created for cards, boxes and notepaper.

The stencil is cut and prepared in exactly the same manner as that used for any other surface, although the application of adhesive spray must be particularly light and the stencil brush should be almost dry to avoid any possibility of bleeding.

Because most varieties of paper absorb so little paint, it is important to ensure that the bristles of the brush are very firm and hit the paper at an angle of 90°. To prevent the bristles from splaying, wrap masking tape around them so that only about 5 mm of the bristles protrude.

I have used just about every kind of paint on paper and have learned to avoid craft paints because they tend to spoil the brushes and dry so completely flat. PVA on paper is also not a very good idea as it is simply too wet.

Fabric paints, aerosol spray paints and paint creams all work well. Spray paints, in particular, look wonderful on paper – very delicate and airy.

Choose a fairly heavy, good quality paper on which to stencil, as it will be more absorbent. For a sophisticated, co-ordinated look, matching envelopes can also be made, using the envelope stencil template at the back of the book. If you are really ambitious, you might even consider creating an entire range of personalised stationery for yourself.

EMBOSSING

Stencils can also be used to emboss the paper – traditionally these would be brass stencils but I have found that acetate stencils work just as well. Paper embossing adds a rich, textured effect to cards and invitations, and is very simple to achieve. To use your stencil for embossing, no adhesive spray is necessary. Choose a fairly heavy paper and attach your stencil to it with a little masking tape. Turn over so that the paper is uppermost. Place both the paper and stencil against a light source – either a window or a lightbox if you have one. You will be able to see the outline of the stencil through the paper.

With an embossing tool – an empty ballpoint pen or a fine knitting needle will do, even a blunt needle if the openings are very fine – trace the outline of the stencil. The reverse side of the paper will have a raised surface with the design embossed on it. This can either be coloured using the stencil (this time secured to the front of the card), left plain or embellished with an embossing powder for a shiny effect.

If you are using a dark-coloured paper, the stencil will not be visible through the paper and you will have to blind emboss. Rub your embossing tool with moderate pressure over the entire area of the hidden stencil – this will reveal the openings in the design, which can then be traced with the embossing tool. Tracing around the square edge of your stencil will create a raised frame around the design.

STENCILLING ON WOOD

Any wooden surface that is properly prepared, or is in good condition, is ideal for stencilling. Wooden floors look lovely when stencilled and give a room a cottage feel. To add interest, the stencilling can be used to demarcate different areas of the room or to define the borders of spaces that are used for certain functions. For instance, a large open-plan area could be divided up into sitting and dining areas by the application of a stencilled border.

Articles of wooden furniture can be enhanced by a pretty motif or border. Wooden chests that are used as children's toy boxes or linen chests are good subjects for beginners. Small cupboards, tables and chairs can also benefit from a little decoration. If the paintwork on the item is in good condition and has not been sealed, you can stencil it and then apply a sealer or varnish to protect the finish. Any type of paint may be used as long as it is compatible with the existing base coat.

However, if the existing paintwork on an item is in poor condition, you will have to strip the wood and sand it down before beginning any work. The finished result will only be as good as the surface you are working on, so thorough preparation is important. Remove any handles or knobs and repair any loose hinges or joints before painting.

If you want to paint an unfinished wooden item, first apply one coat of universal undercoat, followed either by two coats of the desired colour or a paint effect of your choice. The stencil can then be applied and finished with varnish or sealant.

New, unfinished wood that is smoothly sanded can be stencilled on directly and finished with two coats of an appropriate sealer. Wooden floors need to be sanded with a floor-sanding machine – these can usually be hired from a tool hire company. They will also be able to supply the sandpaper in different grades to fit the machine. You will need to sand with a rough, medium and fine grit to achieve a really smooth, even finish. The sanding is neither difficult nor terribly strenuous – rather like cutting the lawn – but it does make a huge mess of sawdust, so use a paper face mask to reduce the amount of dust you inhale. Sweep the floor really well and vacuum before you embark on the stencilling.

STENCILLING WITH BRONZE POWDERS

I use an adaptation of an old technique much used in decoration of tin and papier mâché items by the ancient Chinese in their lacquer work. Bronze powders, also called pigment powders, are applied to a tacky, varnished surface with a pad of velvet to imitate more costly, gold and silver leaf finishes. However, the varnish has to be exactly at the right stage of stickiness to ensure a good result, which can be rather nerve wracking, so I have adapted the process to simplify it for a perfect finish.

Paint the item you wish to stencil with one coat of a universal undercoat and leave to dry overnight. Thereafter, paint two coats of the desired colour and leave to dry.

Spray the reverse of the stencil you wish to use with adhesive spray and fix the stencil to the article. Using a small sponge, dab a little water-based glaze through the stencil onto the wooden surface. With the stencil still in position and using small, flat brushes, immediately apply a little of the dry bronze powder through the stencil over the glaze. Remove the stencil and clean it before the next application as the glaze will bleed under it, onto the back of the stencil.

Leave to dry overnight. Excess powder may be wiped off with a cloth when the glaze is completely dry.

Despite their name, bronze powders are actually very fine, almost dust-like powders of different metals such as copper and zinc. As the metal powders tarnish over a period of time, they need to be sandwiched between layers of varnish or other suitable fixatives, to retain their sheen, therefore paint one coat of a protective varnish (preferably with a sunblock) to seal.

STENCILLING ON WALLS

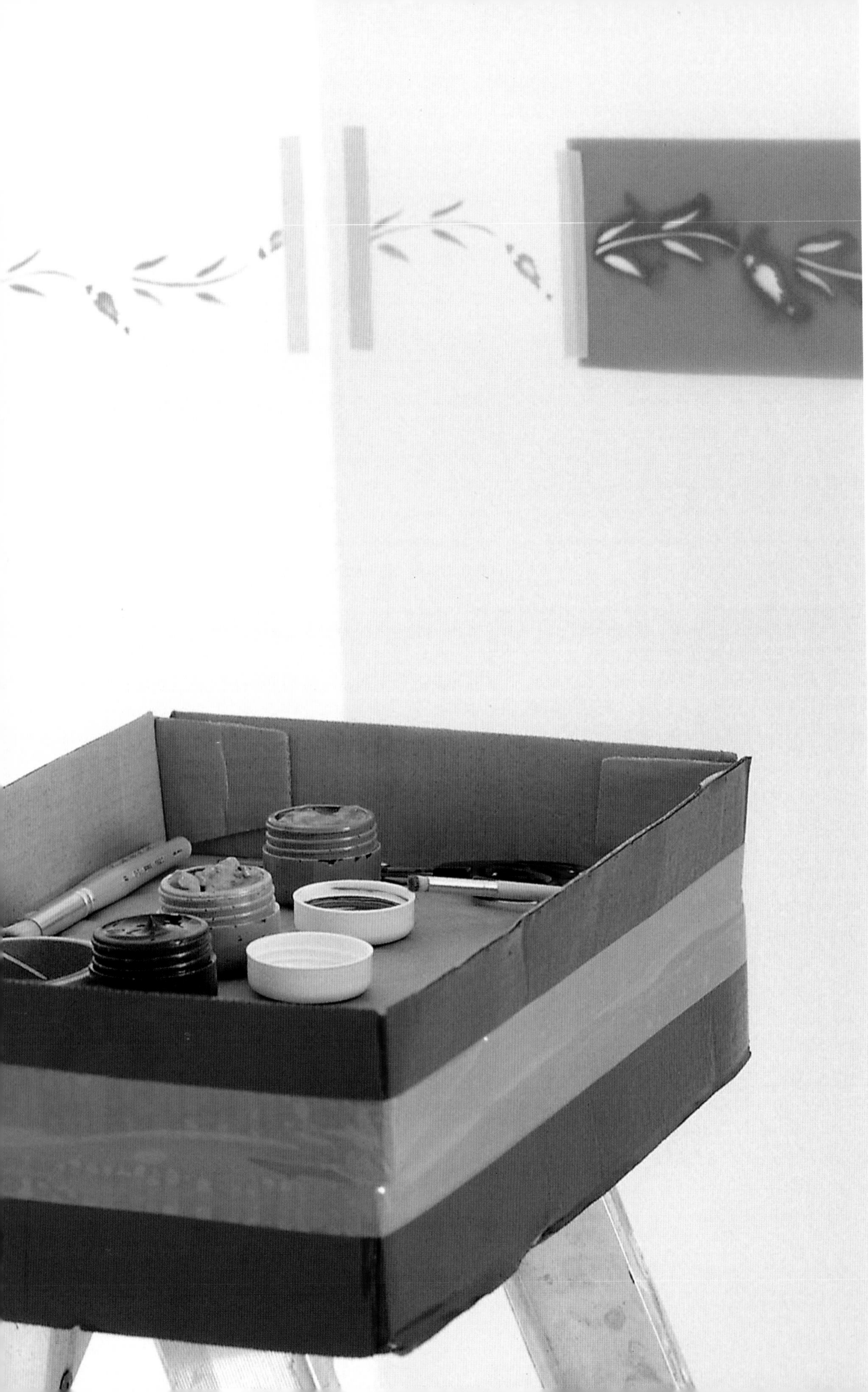

Stencilling the walls of a room can change the entire feel of the room dramatically. Depending on where the stencil is positioned, it can also visually alter the proportions of a space. For example, a border right around a room at waist height draws the room in, making it appear smaller and the ceiling lower, while a border at the same height in a passage elongates the space and makes it seem longer.

The proportions of a stencil are vital so that it does not dominate the room or have the opposite effect and become lost in the space. It is always wise to place the stencil in question on a large piece of card or paper and then tape it to the wall. This will not only allow you to visualise the final result, but also to check your colour choice at the same time. Try to link the colours to other items in the room; muted, soft colours are often far more successful than bright, hard ones.

Stencilling looks best on a broken wall surface – one with shade variations e.g. a wall painted with limewash or where a paint technique has been applied – as it then seems to blend into the paint and not stand out too much. A subtle touch looks far better than one that screams at you. The many different paint techniques are easy to master and add so much to the final result.

How the paint will behave on the actual surface of the wall is always difficult to judge until you start stencilling. The ideal surface is ultra smooth and slightly absorbent, but I have yet to find a perfect wall. Inevitably, you will encounter lumps and bumps, uneven plaster and walls that are not straight. The actual paint on the wall also plays a role in the final result. The silk or satin sheen PVAs provide a lovely working surface, but it's best to avoid high-gloss enamel paint surfaces unless you are using aerosol spray paints.

If you are stencilling close to the ceiling, follow the cornice line even if it is not 100% level, as this is the line that your eye will follow around the room. Ensuring that a border stencil is equidistant from the edge of your stencil material will provide you with a consistent depth guide and also make positioning the stencil much simpler. In the case of a dado stencil, measure up from the floor to find your line and mark lightly with a pencil.

You might find that, in addition to an application of adhesive spray, you will need to apply masking tape to help bear the weight of the stencil and hold it in place. If the wall surface is flaky, first stick the masking tape to a fabric surface such as an old T-shirt to pick up some fluff to prevent it from pulling the paint off the wall.

Keep your paints at a convenient height; if you are working at waist height, use a small table to keep all your materials at a comfortable level. Bending up and down each time you change paints and brushes is good exercise but it can be exhausting. If you are working on a ladder it is a good idea to tape two shallow cardboard boxes such as beer can trays, bottoms together, so that one box fits over the top of your ladder and the other holds all your paints and brushes.

Keep a few ear buds and a damp cloth handy for emergency clean-ups – any spills must be wiped off immediately and watch out for grubby fingers! Also have some of the background paint and a small flat paintbrush available for any emergency touch ups.

Corners can be a bit awkward and bending the stencil to fit often results in messy blotches. To avoid corner problems, the easiest solution is to run a strip of masking tape down both sides of the corner and just stencil over it. The tape can then be removed and the resulting break will be barely noticeable.

Begin your border behind the door – if you have any nervous beginnings they will not be too apparent.

Wall stencils do not need a protective finish unless they are at hand height because the temptation to touch the stencilling seems too difficult to resist for most people. Acrylic paints are very tough and can take normal wiping down occasionally. I have used both fabric paints and PVA in a bathroom without problems. Avoid any cleaning products that contain alcohol, however, as they will break down the paints.

A question that I have been asked more than any other and which I have always had difficulty in answering is, 'How do you apply stencilling onto tiles and other glazed surfaces?'

Of course, if you are a potter or have access to a kiln, it is a simple matter to sponge the paints onto your tiles, then glaze and fire them, but I am referring to someone who wants to smarten up their bathroom with a border on their tiles or wanting to personalise a plate.

Well, at last I have a solution that works easily and is accessible to anyone. The recent development of

tile primers by the paint manufacturers is the breakthrough. Tile primer is painted directly onto the tile, either *in situ* or before tiling. The primer will remain white and will block out the existing colour of the tile.

To stencil a border around a bathroom with existing tiles, first determine the width of your border and run a line of masking tape right around the tiles to the required width. Apply a coat of tile primer and leave to dry.

Any paint effect may then be applied onto the tile, which has been given an absorbent surface. Dilute about four tablespoons of your chosen PVA colour in one cup of water and mix. This wash can be applied with a dragging effect using a dry paintbrush, or as a colourwash using a pad of cloth and rubbing the paint on in a circular motion. Alternatively, you could just paint it straight from the tin.

Cut and prepare your stencil with adhesive spray. Position your stencil and paint, using stencil brushes. Because you are working on a hard surface that is not very absorbent, ensure that the brushes are almost dry – to avoid bleeding. I usually use the paint that sticks to the lid of the tin, as it is always a little thicker.

Stencil directly over the joins in the tiles. If you have messed paint over the grouting in between the tiles, fix it with a grouting pen, available from hardware shops.

Apply two coats of water-based glaze in either a matt or gloss finish, to seal. The tiles may be wiped clean with a damp cloth or sponge, but avoid harsh abrasives.

The same process may be used for plates and other ceramic items, but they would not be suitable for household use and should be used for decorative purposes only.

KILN-FIRED CERAMICS

'Blanks' or unglazed bisqueware (formed clay that has undergone the first firing) are readily obtainable from pottery suppliers. They also provide underglaze paints, glazes and plenty of advice.

You will need access to a kiln to complete a project such as this but many of the craft shops now offer a firing service, especially if they offer pottery painting classes. Alternatively, your local pottery supplier should be able to put you in touch with someone who can fire items for you.

Stencils for use on unglazed pottery are cut from brown paper or newspaper and then dampened so that they follow the shape of the item and cling closely to it. Unfortunately, although newspaper works very well, it can only be used once; you can try cutting more than one stencil at one time by layering the newspaper. Brown paper is also good and if you use a strong paper, the stencil can be used a number of times.

Paints used for colouring ceramics are called 'underglaze' and, as the name suggests, they are applied to the bisqueware before glazing. The problem is that their colours are quite different before and after firing. Try to find someone who is knowledgeable about this to advise you. Most pottery supply shops will have samples of the colours once they have been fired to give you an idea of the final result.

The big bonus with stencilling on ceramics is that you get not only one, but two chances to fix any spills or bleeding that might occur.

The first is immediately after you have applied the underglaze paint. Scrape any obvious errors away with a sharp tool. This is fine if you can actually see the mistake, but often the colour of the paint is such that these are not easily visible. For example, a midnight blue paint might be light pink in its unfired state and will not show up very well against the clay before firing. In this case a bisque firing before the article is glazed will allow the true colour to show up any irregularities and can still be removed with a sharp tool before the glaze is applied.

If the article is intended for food use, be sure to check that any glaze that is applied is lead free. Purely decorative items can have any type of glaze, but all functional ware MUST have lead-free glazes. The glaze will render the item impermeable to liquids as well as giving it a protective layer.

Underglaze paints for stencilling purposes that are recommended by Karen Peters, who is an expert in pottery and glazes, include the more expensive, imported varieties. On the positive side, however, they require only one application for a good depth of colour, thereby minimising any bleeding. Details may be added with a brush after the initial stencilling.

STENCILLING ON SKIN

Just to show the fun and extreme versatility of stencilling, I have included the application of temporary tattoos with the aid of stencils, which has become very fashionable recently.

These stencils are used without adhesive spray, just being held firmly in position. The colour is sprayed on with an airbrush and the paints normally have isopropyl alcohol to thin them down, so although safe for use on the face, care should be taken near eyes, nose and mouth.

As not everyone has access to an airbrush, I have discovered another method to achieve the same effect. There are many types of face paint available on the market and by applying these with a stencil brush, a very good result can be obtained, although not as good as those sprayed with an airbrush.

Pick a face paint that has the consistency of thick, creamy lipstick – these are normally sold in little tubs – as the more liquid ones are not suitable for stencilling. Temporary tattoos require only a very thin layer of paint on the surface of the skin and any clothing or straps covering them will cause them to wear off very quickly. Sweat also causes them to break down, so apply a little baby powder quite often. These paints can cause staining of clothing.

1 Clean the skin around the area where the stencil is to be applied with alcohol to remove any dirt and natural oils.

2 When the skin is completely dry, place the stencil in position and hold down firmly.

3 Apply the paint with brushes (see opposite).

4 Remove when complete and leave to dry.

5 Pat a little baby powder onto the tattoo, which will set it and help protect it.

6 The tattoos may be removed by using alcohol or baby oil on a piece of cotton wool or tissue.

YOU WILL NEED

- small bottle 70% isopropyl alcohol or rubbing alcohol/alcohol swabs
- face paints – usually available at craft or toyshops (the Siggi™ brand is good)
- small stencil brushes

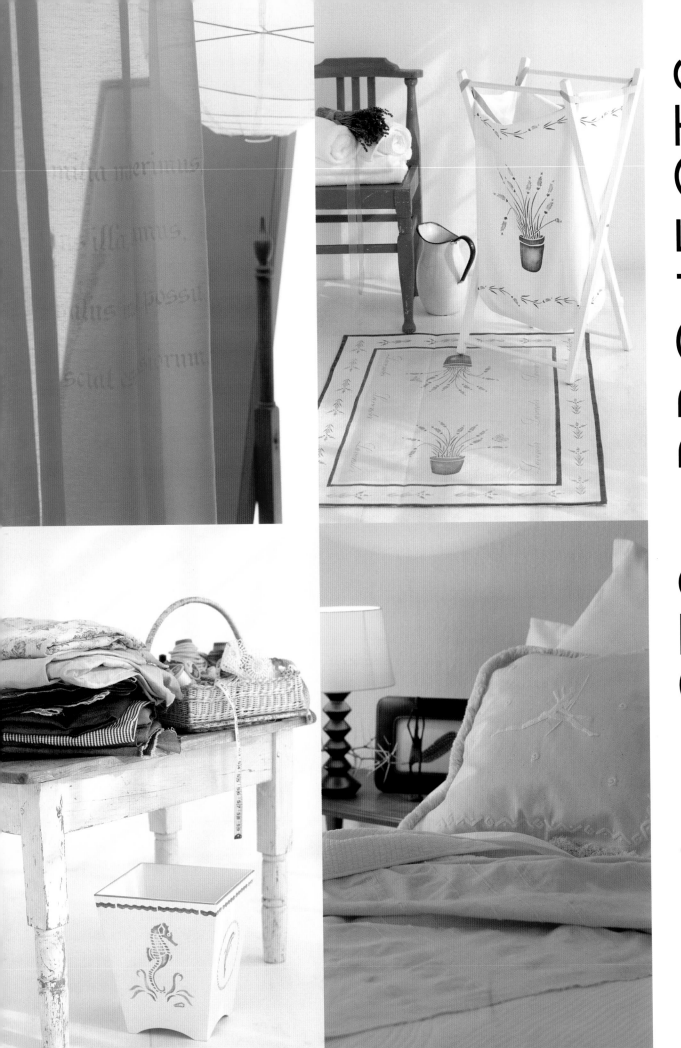

I have a lot of fun using stencils on a variety of different surfaces, using a range of media. All the projects featured here work well – they have been tried and tested many times. However, do not feel restricted to using a certain stencil for a certain project – the designs are suitable for any project.

Before beginning a project, I suggest that you read carefully the section covering the techniques used on the surface you will be working on, as I have included many tips and hints that will save you time and prevent problems. Do not feel that you have to follow my colour suggestions or instructions slavishly – they are there merely as guidelines to help you unlock your own style.

LEMON AND OLIVE TABLECLOTH

TWO-LAYERED STENCIL

This fresh design is a classic and perfect for summer meals outdoors. It looks good on a white background and, as with all the projects, the colours are merely recommended and do not need to be copied slavishly. Try to achieve a natural realism, especially with fruit, as I think this looks best. Matching table napkins using either the olives or a lemon add the finishing touch. The olives may be used alone as a separate stencil, on a co-ordinated item.

1 Determine the size cloth you will need by measuring the surface of your table and adding 20 cm to all sides for the overhang. An easy way to cut a round cloth is to fold your square into four, then, using a piece of string the length of which is the radius of the circle you require, attach a pencil to one end and, using the point of the square as a pivot, draw a line at the end of the string. Cut along this line and open out the circle.

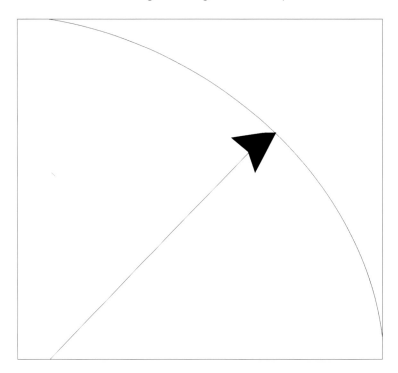

YOU WILL NEED

- hopsack linen or white cotton to size
- adhesive spray
- fabric paints in each of the following colours: light yellow, sunflower yellow, khaki, chocolate brown, olive green, hunter's green, black
- 4 small stencil brushes
- 3 medium stencil brushes
- plastic shield with curve
- fabric liner in black

2 A tip to achieve a flat hem on a round cloth is to hem the cloth as normal and then to run an additional row of stitching about 2 mm from the edge of the fabric but sewing with the wrong side of the cloth facing up. This will ensure that the hem lies completely flat.

3 Using a photocopier, resize the lemon and olive design at the back of the book to the size required and print two copies. For this tablecloth I used the design to fit on an A4-sized sheet of paper.

4 Number each copy and fix, right side facing up, onto a sheet of acetate. Beginning with sheet one, cut out all the areas marked '1'. Be sure to cut on the outside of the lines. Proceed to the next sheet and cut out all the areas marked '2'. Do not forget to cut out the four registration holes on each sheet.

5 Number the front of each stencil with a felt-tip pen in the top right-hand corner before removing the paper sheet. Spray the back of each stencil with adhesive spray; check that you are spraying the back by ensuring that the numbers on each stencil face the top, or you may end up with stencils sprayed on different sides.

6 Decide where you want your stencil border to be and position stencil 1. Using pins, mark the four registration holes.

7 Using light yellow, stencil the lemons (leaving the central area white) and their leaves.

8 Apply sunflower yellow around the edges of the lemons. Use a touch of olive green to highlight one side of the lemons. With the plastic shield, create curves at the top and bottom of the lemons. Apply olive green over the yellow on the leaves. Use hunter's green around the edges of the leaves, then with the shield create a vein down the centre of each leaf.

9 Stencil the olives in black leaving a white area in the centre. Apply chocolate brown to the twigs. Remove stencil 1.

10 Position stencil 2, lining up the registration points with the four inserted pins. Complete the last lemon leaf as before. Stencil the olive leaves in khaki and edge with hunter's green. Use the shield to create veins. Fill in the remaining stems with chocolate brown. Remove stencil 2.

11 Use the two pins on the righthand side of the print to position stencil 1 for the next repeat and insert two more pins in the vacant holes. Paint stencil 1 as before.

12 Black fabric liner could be used to fill in the stems of olives.

13 When dry, iron well on the reverse side or fix paint according to instructions.

Once the stencil has been correctly positioned, pins should be inserted to mark the four registration holes.

BERRIES AND CHERRIES DECKCHAIR COVER

A bright, cheerful deckchair invites you to enjoy the fruits of your labours – the epitome of summer relaxation. You can often find old wooden deckchairs at junk shops or auctions – you may even have a couple with rotting canvas covers in your own garage. I found a broken one discarded at the side of the road; some glue and paint later and I had a lovely blue chair with a dolphin cover – all for a few rands!

Remove the cover and note how it is attached to the wood as you do so. If possible, use the old cover as a pattern for the replacement. The best canvas to use is 510-g 'cotton duck', as this will bear the weight of a person. If the frame needs attention or sanding down and painting, do those repairs before attaching the new cover. Paint sanded wood with a good quality wood varnish to protect against sun damage.

This deckchair featured here has a built-in shade awning that's also been stencilled. You could also stencil cushions to match, using the fruit motifs in a larger size.

1 Cut the canvas to size, then determine where your design should be positioned. Use pins to mark this position or mark the canvas lightly in pencil.

2 Make three photocopies of the Berries and Cherries design (at the back of the book) to the size you require; I used the design with a length of 32 cm. Number each copy.

3 Secure each copy to a sheet of stencil material and number the front of each sheet '1', '2' or '3' with a felt-tip pen in the top right-hand corner. Cut out all the areas marked '1' on the first sheet, remembering to cut on the outside of the lines and to cut out the four registration points. Do the same for sheets 2 and 3. Remove the paper copies.

YOU WILL NEED

- white cotton duck 510-g canvas as required
- adhesive spray
- fabric paints in the following colours: red, maroon, sunflower yellow, orange, olive green, hunter's green, violet, chocolate brown, flesh, terracotta
- black fabric liner
- 8 small stencil brushes
- 2 medium stencil brushes
- binding or fringing for edges (if desired)
- wooden deck chair frame
- upholstery tacks and decorative studs
- plastic shield with curve

4 Spray the back of each stencil with adhesive spray. Check that you are spraying the back – the numbers on each stencil should face up otherwise you may end up with a confusing lot of stencils with adhesive sprayed on different sides.

5 Position stencil 1 and mark the registration holes with pins or pencil. Using olive green, lightly stencil all leaves. Use hunter's green around the edges of the leaves and create a vein down the leaf centres using a curved shield. Apply sunflower yellow for the gooseberries, leaving an area of light in the centre, then do the same for the cherries using red. Surround the cherries with maroon. For the youngberries, stencil lightly with violet. Remove stencil 1.

6 Use registration pins to position stencil 2. Stencil the leaves as before and use hunter's green for stems and flower centres. Finish cherries as before and stencil the strawberries in the same manner. For the gooseberry casings, use a little flesh over the entire area with a tiny amount of terracotta at the edges, using the shield to create the casing lines. Remove stencil 2.

7 Position stencil 3 and finish the leaves and casing areas as described previously. For the flowers apply sunflower yellow with a little edging of orange. Use violet for the youngberry nodules and chocolate brown for the strawberry seeds. Remove stencil 3 and position stencil 1 for the next repeat, using the two pins at the bottom of the finished print and inserting two more pins in the vacant registration holes.

8 To print the stencil mirror image on the other side of the cover, clean the stencils and allow them to dry thoroughly before spraying the other side with spray adhesive. Use as before.

9 When all stencilling is complete, the stalks for the cherries can be added with a black fabric liner

10 Finish the edges either with a binding trim or fringing, because hemming the thick canvas is impossible without an industrial sewing machine.

11 When you have completed the cover, attach it to the frame with upholstery tacks and decorative studs, at the same time stretching the canvas quite tightly as you do so. The cover may be protected with Scotchguard™ if required.

12 Pour a well-deserved cold drink and try out your new chair!

LAVENDER FLOORCLOTH AND LAUNDRY BAG

Floorcloths were the forerunners of modern-day linoleum. They are ideal for children's rooms, holiday houses and kitchens as they are tough, hard wearing and simply need a wipe down to clean. Contrary to expectation, the paint does not crack on a floorcloth and it is quite flexible, even allowing for rolled storage.

When buying canvas, ask the store assistant to roll it up and not to fold it as fold marks take a long time to ease out. All camping equipment specialist shops stock canvas.

The floorcloth featured opposite was made to match the laundry basket and is used as a bath mat.

FLOORCLOTH ▪ FLOORCLOTH

In order to avoid stitching through more than one layer of canvas, I use the method below to finish the edges of the floorcloth. Use a leather needle for your sewing machine and, if in doubt as to whether your machine can cope with the canvas, take the floorcloth to an upholsterer to stitch it on an industrial machine.

1 Pin the longer lengths of tape to the long sides of the canvas, 5 mm from the edge. Leave 3 cm of tape to overlap at the corners. Repeat with the shorter sides. Sew along pinned seam.

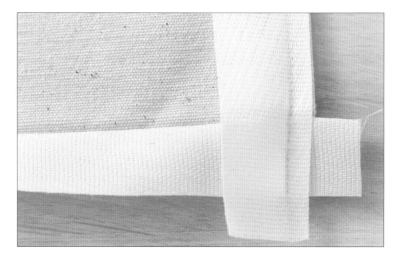

YOU WILL NEED

- 1 m x 80 cm white cotton duck 510 g canvas (or size as required)
- 3.84 m x 2 cm-wide tape in matching colour, cut into two lengths of 1.06 m and two lengths of 86 cm
- 1 litre universal undercoat in white
- 1 litre PVA in white
- paintbrushes
- masking tape
- fabric paints in the following colours: olive green, faded denim, jacaranda, terracotta, chocolate brown
- a small pot of PVA in pale lilac
- adhesive spray
- 3 small stencil brushes
- 2 medium stencil brushes
- 1 litre protective varnish (with sunblock) in a suede finish

2 Turn the tape over to the other side of the canvas and press the canvas down so that it folds under at the stitching. Tuck the corner allowances in neatly and stitch the free edges of the tape.

3 Paint the entire floorcloth with a generous coat of universal undercoat. The canvas will soak up a considerable amount of paint so ensure that it is well covered. Leave to dry overnight.

4 Paint the floorcloth with one coat of white PVA and leave to dry.

5 Stick masking tape 1 cm from the edge of the cloth. Mark 14 cm from the edge of the canvas and draw a pencil line right around the cloth. Secure two rows of masking tape 0.5 cm on each side of the pencil line thus leaving a gap of 1 cm between the two rows of masking tape. Paint a line around the outside of the cloth and between the rows of tape using a small flat brush and olive green fabric paint.

6 Mix about four teaspoons of pale lilac paint with four tablespoons of water and paint the rectangle in the centre of the cloth. Carefully remove all masking tape and leave to dry.

7 Photocopy the lavender designs at the back of the book to the desired size. (I used the lavender in the pot with a height of 33 cm and the curved lavender border with a length of 11 cm.) The lettering used on the floorcloth is the same as that used for the laundry basket and is Kunstler font, cut as a two-part stencil 18.5 cm in length.

8 Attach the photocopies to your stencil material, cut out the designs and spray the back of the stencils with adhesive spray.

9 Centre the lavender sprig in the border strip created by the two green lines. Using faded denim paint and a small brush, lightly stencil the lavender sprig, but leaving the area in the middle open. Edge with jacaranda. Stencil all the foliage olive green.

10 Remove the stencil and continue all around the border as before.

11 Position the lavender pot stencil. With a medium brush, cover most of the pot with terracotta leaving an open area in the centre. Edge with chocolate brown. Stencil the flowers in the same manner as the sprig (in step 9) and stencil the leaves olive green.

12 Position part 1 of the lettering, then stencil in jacaranda and repeat for part 2.

13 If you wish, the little butterfly and bee stencils may be used to add interest.

14 Leave to dry and cover with one coat of protective varnish. Leave to dry overnight.

LAUNDRY BAG ▪ LAUNDRY BAG

The colours of the lavender flowers together with their grey-green foliage look cool and crisp against white. I have used the design on a laundry basket and a canvas floorcloth that can double as a bathmat.

1 Cut bull denim according to instructions on the opposite page. Mark a line with pencil, 20 cm from the top edge of the fabric. Pin, then sew the tape along this line as follows: attach tape for 22 cm from side edge, make an 18-cm loop of the tape and pin along the line for 40 cm, make another 18-cm loop and pin for a further 20 cm. Make a final 18-cm loop and pin long the rest of the line. Sew as pinned.

YOU WILL NEED

- 1 m white bull denim cloth (or a heavy cotton)
- 2 m (2 cm-wide) tape in matching colour
- adhesive spray
- fabric paints in the following colours: faded denim, jacaranda, olive green, terracotta, chocolate brown
- 2 m cord
- wooden laundry frame
- 3 small stencil brushes
- 2 medium stencil brushes

2 Photocopy the lavender design at the back of the book to desired size (I used the lavender in the pot with a height of 33 cm and the lavender border spray with a length of 12 cm). If you wish to make a stencil of the same lavender lettering that I have used on the laundry bag, I used a Kunstler script and cut a two-part lettering stencil.

3 Attach the photocopies to your stencil material, cut out the designs and spray the back of the stencils with adhesive.

4 Position the lavender pot in the centre of the fabric area, with the extended bottom edge allowing enough space for the placement of a border above and below it. Using the faded denim and the smaller brushes, lightly stencil the flowers leaving the centre area open. Edge with jacaranda. Stencil all foliage in olive green.

5 With a medium brush, cover most of the pot with terracotta leaving an open area in the centre. Edge with chocolate brown. Remove stencil.

6 Position the border stencil below the tape and apply faded denim and jacaranda paints as before. Finish leaves and stem in olive green (see left). Repeat the border along the top and bottom edges.

7 Fix fabric paint with an iron or dry heat.

TO MAKE UP ▪ TO MAKE UP ▪ TO MAKE UP ▪ TO MAKE UP

1 Turn 1 cm under, along the top edge, and iron the fold.

2 With right sides together, sew up 1.5-cm side seam, making a final loop of the remaining tape.

3 Sew the short sides of the extended bottom section to the main body of the bag to form the sides and sew along the side of the extension to the remaining bottom edge.

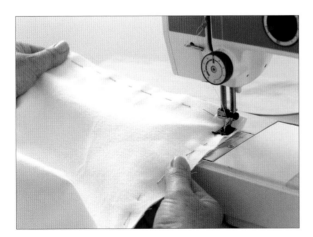

4 Make a 4-cm hem along the top edge, leaving a gap of 2 cm through which to insert a cord.

5 Insert the cord and knot the ends together.

6 Using the tape loops, hang the bag onto a wooden frame.

CUTTING INSTRUCTIONS FOR LAUNDRY BAG

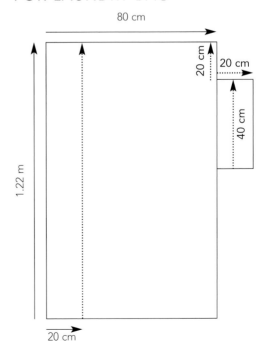

80 cm

1.22 m

20 cm

20 cm

40 cm

20 cm

VELVET EVENING BAGS

At the beginning of the 19th century, Theorem painting or stencilling on velvet was very popular with young ladies of leisure in America. The Theorem apparently referred to the puzzle of placing individual elements of a stencil in such a way as to create a pleasing composition. Typical subjects included fruit and flowers and the end result was often framed as a wall hanging.

Applying stencils onto velvet creates a rich, lustrous result and lends itself to luxury items. White cotton velvet is extremely difficult to find but velour makes a suitable substitute. Unfortunately, the normal fabric paints do not work well on this fabric so oil-based cream paints must be used. These are expensive and take at least ten days to dry so the item must be handled with care after printing. However, oil-based cream paints are easy to use, require very little effort to apply and almost seem to float on the surface of the velour. Butterflies in bright, jewelled colours adorn these easy-to-make evening bags.

1 Cut the velour or velvet and lining as per the cutting diagram.

2 Photocopy the butterfly designs at the back of the book to the required size (I used at ±5 cm).

3 First attach the photocopies to the stencil material, then cut the stencils.

4 Spray the back of the stencils with adhesive spray.

5 Lay out the largest piece of velour or velvet and, leaving at least 6 cm free on one long edge for the hem and cord casing, position the butterflies in a pleasing arrangement.

6 If using white velour, apply the cream paints directly, shading each colour into the other and using gold for the bodies and random swirls. (You will find that very little paint is required.)

7 On a dark fabric, first apply a layer of white opaque paint through the stencils and leave to dry.

8 Reposition the butterfly stencils directly over the white prints and stencil with coloured cream paints.

9 Leave the velour or velvet to dry for about ten days before making up the bag.

YOU WILL NEED

- 30 cm white velour or bottle green velvet
- 30 cm fabric lining
- adhesive spray
- oil-based cream fabric paints in the following colours: gold, turquoise, royal blue, grape, violet
- opaque fabric paint (if you are using the dark velvet) in white
- small piece (±10 cm) of iron-on stiffening material
- 1 m decorative rope for handles, cut in half
- 5 small stencil brushes

TO MAKE UP • TO MAKE UP • TO MAKE UP • TO MAKE UP

1 If you would like to add any beadwork or other trimming, complete this first.

2 Iron stiffening to the back of the base circle with a warm iron.

3 Fold in the short edges of the casing and hem.

4 Fold in the long edges of the casing and pin into position with the bottom edge of the casing 6 cm from the top of the stencilled section, then stitch.

5 Sew the side seam, taking care not to catch it in the edges of the casing.

6 Gather the bottom edge of the main section to fit the stiffened circle. Pin and stitch.

7 Sew the side seam of the fabric lining.

8 Gather the bottom edge of the lining, then attach it to the lining circle, in the same manner as for main section of the bag.

9 Keeping the right sides together, pin and stitch the top edges of the main section of the bag and the lining together.

10 Tuck the lining into the bag, then top stitch the top edge.

11 Thread the cord through the casing and knot.

CUTTING INSTRUCTIONS FOR EVENING BAGS

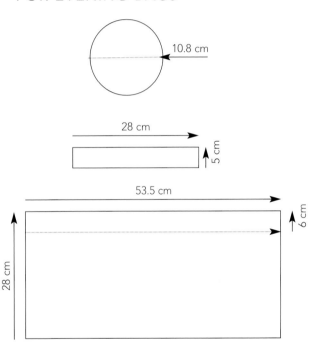

10.8 cm

28 cm

5 cm

53.5 cm

6 cm

28 cm

TOILE STENCIL BLIND

Traditionally toile fabrics feature stylised country designs and for this effect stencilling is ideal. Only one colour is used in the printing and is therefore quick to complete, a bonus as it takes hours to cut the very fine stencils that are required. A traditional room in toile décor has the same design repeated on virtually every surface – walls, soft furnishings and curtains – which I find a little overpowering, so have just used it on a blind.

In this project, scenes of early pioneers in Africa and stencil designs in khaki create a very 'Out of Africa' feel.

YOU WILL NEED

- adhesive spray
- light cream cotton to fit required blind size
- fabric paint in khaki
- medium stencil brush
- lining for blind, if required

1 Photocopy the toile designs at the back of the book to the desired size – if you are unsure of the size, look at toile fabrics in a shop to get an idea.

2 Cut the stencils – this is going to be a time-consuming exercise so put on your favourite CD and relax – you will enjoy the result!

3 Spray the back of the stencils with adhesive spray.

4 Position the stencils randomly on the fabric and stencil using khaki fabric paint.

5 Cure the paint when dry and make up into a blind design of your choice.

GRAPEVINE TABLECLOTH

What would a collection of stencils be without a vine design? And as I live in one of South Africa's wine-producing areas, it is quite fitting to include one. (I have not included an ivy stencil, as there are thousands available.)

This design would look lovely on the walls of a dining room or outside on a verandah, but I have used it on a large tablecloth as I think it makes a beautiful setting for a festive meal, as well as al fresco dining. This is a three-layered stencil and is best printed in rich, jewel colours.

1 Hem the two short ends of the fabric and iron into half, lengthways, and then iron again half across the width of the material. This will create guidelines to follow when you position the central area of the tablecloth.

2 Photocopy three copies of the grapevine design at the back of the book to the required size; number the copies '1', '2' and '3'. (I used the design with a length of 47 cm.)

3 Attach each photocopy to a sheet of stencil material, then number them '1', '2' and '3' respectively in the top right-hand corners. Cut out all the sections marked '1' on the sheet marked '1', not forgetting to cut the four registration points as well. Remember to cut on the outside of the lines to ensure overlapping in the joins of the design. Repeat for sheets 2 and 3. The veins for all the leaves are cut on stencil 3.

4 Spray the back of each stencil with adhesive spray, making sure the numbers on each stencil face the top otherwise you may end up with a confusing set of stencils with the adhesive sprayed on different sides.

5 Position stencil 1 in the left-hand corner of your tablecloth, allowing 5 cm from the edges of the design to the edge of the fabric. Mark registration points with pins.

6 Using a medium stencil brush and olive green paint, lightly stencil the leaves, leaving the centre of the leaves a little lighter. Use hunter's green and a small brush to stencil around the edges of the leaves. With a small brush and maroon paint, stencil each grape berry, once again working from the outside of the area in order to leave a light spot in the middle of each fruit. Stencil the twigs in chocolate brown. Remove stencil 1.

YOU WILL NEED

- 2 m white hopsack linen, or required size to fit a table plus a 20-cm overhang all round
- adhesive spray
- fabric paints in the following colours: olive green, hunter's green, maroon, violet, terracotta, chocolate brown
- 2 medium stencil brushes
- 4 small stencil brushes

7 Use registration pins to position stencil 2 and press into place. Print the leaves as before, as well as the spirals, in hunter's green. Stencil the grape berries in violet, again working from the outer edges of each berry. The branches are printed in terracotta then edged in chocolate brown. Remove stencil 2.

8 Use registration pins to position stencil 3 and press into place. Print the last leaf as before and complete the spirals with hunter's green. Also use hunter's green to print the veins over the leaves that have already been stencilled. Print the grape berries first with maroon then edge with violet. Finish the last twig with Chocolate Brown. Remove stencil 3.

9 Position stencil 1 to the right of the completed design using the registration pins, then insert two more pins in the vacant righthand registration holes.

10 Repeat steps 6 to 8, working around the edges of the cloth.

11 Using the ironed lines in the centre of the cloth, mark out an area with pins 30 cm on either side of the centre of the length line and 15 cm on either side of the width line.

12 Use the pinned line as a guide to stencil the central area of the cloth.

13 Cure the paint as per instructions.

NASTURTIUM CUSHION

FOUR-LAYERED STENCIL

Nasturtiums are cheerful flowers and a pleasure to see in the spring or even the late winter when they add warmth to bleak days. This stencil design allows you to enjoy their fresh, citrus colours all year round. Here I have used them on a cushion cover, but they would look equally charming as a border in a bedroom or in a sunny sitting room. Don't be put off by the fact that four layers need to be cut – it is not a difficult design to cut or to print.

1 Cut a piece of linen, 50 x 50 cm, for the front of the cushion cover, and another two pieces, 50 x 28 cm for the back. Stitch the two back pieces together, leaving an opening of 35 cm for the zip.

2 Iron the seam flat and insert the zip. Open the zip.

3 Photocopy four copies of the nasturtium design at the back of the book to the required size. (I used the design with a length of 28 cm.)

4 Attach each copy to a sheet of stencil material and number each sheet in the top right-hand corner '1' to '4'. On sheet 1, cut out all the sections marked '1'. Remember to cut on the outside of the lines and don't forget to cut the four registration points on each sheet. Repeat with sheets 2, 3 and 4.

5 Spray the back of each stencil with adhesive spray, ensuring that the number of the stencil faces up otherwise you may end up with a muddled set of stencils sprayed on different sides.

6 Lay out the front cover of the cushion and, allowing for the seam, position stencil 1. Mark the four registration points with pins.

7 Refer to the design pattern to distinguish between the flowers and leaves of the stencil.

8 Using a medium stencil brush, apply light yellow to all flowers and leaves. Cover the stems and leaves with olive green, leaving a yellow area in the centre. Outline each leaf with a little hunter's green.

YOU WILL NEED

- 50 cm (150 cm-wide) cream hopsack linen or other lightweight cotton
- 35 cm cream zip
- adhesive spray
- 5 small stencil brushes
- 1 medium stencil brush
- fabric paints in the following colours: light yellow, sunflower yellow, orange, red, olive green, hunter's green
- 50 cm fabric lining
- 40 x 40 cm cushion inner

9 Apply sunflower yellow to the edges of the flowers followed by a light touch of orange. Remove stencil 1.

10 Use registration pins to position stencil 2, then print the leaves, flowers and stems in the same manner as previously. Apply hunter's green to the leaf veins. Remove stencil 2.

11 Position stencil 3 with the aid of registration pins and complete as before, applying hunter's green to the seedpods. Remove stencil 3.

12 Position stencil 4 as previously and apply red to the flower detail and olive green to the remaining stem. Remove stencil 4.

13 Secure stencil 1 to the right of the completed design, aligning the two pins with holes in the left of the stencil and inserting another two pins in the righthand registration holes.

14 Complete your design right around the cushion cover and cure the paint, when dry, according to instructions.

TO MAKE UP ▪ TO MAKE UP ▪ TO MAKE UP ▪ TO MAKE UP

I always prefer to line cushion fronts because not only do they look more professional, but it also makes it easier to insert the cushion inner once the fronts have been lined.

1 Lay the cushion front over the lining fabric, with the printed side up. Lay the back portion of the cover on top, with the right sides together.

2 Pin and stitch a 1-cm seam around the square.

3 Turn the cover right side out (through the zip opening) and iron.

4 If you like, pin and stitch a square 5 cm from the cushion edges. Press and insert the cushion inner.

POETRY VOILE CURTAINS

I have always admired the manner in which Eastern cultures use their beautiful flowing scripts as a decorative element in their architecture. We have so many different fonts available today with the aid of computers that it is a simple matter to design with lettering.

This project combines the use of decorative lettering with poetry so that all your favourite bits of poetry can be with you in a room. It is not necessary to copy out entire poems – only use the lines that appeal to you or that have remained in your memory from school days. Other ideas could be to use inspirational sayings or affirmations that appeal to you.

Using the same font throughout creates a unified effect and a white on cream colour scheme permits the letters to become visible as the fabric moves and the light alters. Sheer curtains with airy, delicate patterns that hang in filmy folds have come onto the market in recent years. Most of these fabrics, with the exception of muslin, are made from synthetic fibres and normal water-based fabric paints just sink right through them. However, oil-based cream paints or aerosol spray paints will print onto sheers with beautiful, subtle results.

The cardinal rule when stencilling sheers is to have an absorbent backing to stencil on and to ensure that it is clean every time you lay the fabric onto it, otherwise you will pick up every bit of paint that has gone through the sheer fabric onto your table with each new section you print. Newsprint spread over the table and renewed each time you move the fabric will serve the purpose, provided you do not pick up excess printing ink from the paper.

multa merinus,

ns illa, imus,

alius mb possit,

scut essiorum.

1 Select your lines of poetry (or other inspirational verse), then print them out from your computer in your favourite font. (For this project I used Parchment font, a lovely flowing script with plenty of embellishment.)

2 On a photocopier (or at a print shop), enlarge the printed poems to the size you want. You will need to enlarge the script over an A3 or even A2 (two A3 sheets) sheet of paper or it will be too small and difficult to cut.

3 Rather large pieces of stencil material will be required so join two or more sheets together with masking tape, butting the edges together to make smooth joins.

4 Cut out the poem stencils – it will take quite a while depending on the number of different verses or phrases you decide to use.

5 Lightly spray the back of each stencil with adhesive spray and position the writing on the fabric, taking care to keep the script straight. Completely frame the script with newspaper and secure with masking tape.

6 With a gentle, pumping action, spray the stencil. Because your index finger will tire fairly quickly, as quite a bit of force is needed to release the paint, rest frequently and build up light layers of paint rather than try to cover in one go.

7 Repeat the process with the other sections of poetry and scatter gold stars using a star-shaped stencil, if you wish, with a gold-coloured cream paint.

8 Make up the curtains using filament thread for invisible seams.

9 Attach curtain tape of your choice and hang.

10 These curtains will be fully washable.

YOU WILL NEED

- masking tape
- adhesive spray
- aerosol spray paint in white
- oil-based cream paint in gold (optional)
- cream voile to fit windows
- curtain tape in desired style
- filament thread for invisible seams

Da mi basia mille, deinde centum,

dein mille altera, dein secunda centum,

deinde usque altera mille, deinde centum.

Dein, cum milia multa fecerimus,

conturbabimus illa, ne sciamus,

aut ne quis malus invidere possit,

cum tantum sciat esse basiorum.

ROCK ART CUSHION COVER

The cream-on-cream colour scheme looks sophisticated and is used here with rock art designs and African borders. An assortment of cushions complement a minimalist interior, possibly with a touch of gold braiding for a stylish finish.

YOU WILL NEED

- 55 cm (150 cm-wide) cream bull denim
- 55 x 55 cm piece of fabric lining
- 45 cm cream zip
- adhesive spray
- puff paint in cream
- medium stencil brush
- 2 m cream fringing
- 50 x 50 cm cushion inner

1 Cut one piece of bull denim, 55 x 55 cm, for the front of the cushion cover and two pieces, 55 x 28 cm each, for the back. Stitch the two back pieces together leaving an opening of 45 cm for the zip.

2 Iron the seam flat and insert the zip. Open the zip.

3 Select a size for one of the African border and Bushman Hunter stencils at the back of the book. Photocopy and enlarge the chosen designs. Secure the copies to sheets of stencil material and cut the stencils.

4 Spray the back of each of the stencils with adhesive spray.

5 Position your stencils and paint a fairly thick application of the cream puff paint.

6 When the stencilling is complete, leave to dry completely.

7 With an iron on a 'cotton' setting, slowly pass the iron over the wrong side of the cushion front. Indentations will form as the paint puffs up. *Do not iron again.*

TO MAKE UP ▪ TO MAKE UP

1 Lay the cushion front over the lining, with the printed side facing up. Pin the fringing around the edges of the cushion front, ensuring that the 'rough' side of the fringing faces in.

2 Position the back of the cushion cover on top of the cushion front, with the right sides together. Pin and stitch a 1-cm seam around the square.

3 Turn the cushion cover inside out through the zip opening.

4 Press the edges of the seam only, to flatten, and insert the cushion inner.

ANIMAL PRINT SHOPPING BAGS

With the recent ban on free plastic shopping bags in our country, shoppers have had to change their habits and cloth shopping bags have become very popular. Sturdy, spacious bags with strong handles are a necessity and make very welcome gifts. This bag is cut from one piece of fabric, requires the minimum of sewing and can be run up in a matter of minutes. The squared bottom also makes it suitable as a book bag. All the stencil designs in this book are suitable for the bag and a variety are shown. Refer to the printing instructions for each design.

1 Cut the fabric as per the cutting instructions below.

2 Fold over 3.5 cm from the top edge for the hem, then stitch.

3 The area inside the dotted square on the cutting diagram corresponds to the front of the bag, so if you have chosen a large motif, place it here.

4 For these bags I used the animal designs enlarged to an A4 size and the skin print borders 6 cm wide

5 The stencils are cut and prepared with adhesive spray on the back of each stencil.

6 For the zebra bag, place the skin border stencil at the top of the bag and simply apply black fabric paint through the stencil. For a really good result, ensure that all of the exposed fabric is well covered, therefore it is possible that more that one application of paint may be necessary.

7 Position the zebra design, then stencil with black fabric paint in the same manner as for the border. Don't forget to cure the fabric paint when dry.

8 For the giraffe bag, place the skin border near the top of the bag and proceed as in step 6. A bit of shading makes this border look quite realistic.

9 First apply sunshine yellow paint over most of the skin markings leaving a small area of fabric exposed in the centre of each section.

YOU WILL NEED

- 0.5 m cream bull denim (150 cm wide) for each bag
- adhesive spray
- fabric paints in black for zebra bag; sunshine yellow, terracotta, chocolate brown and olive for giraffe bag
- 1 large stencil brush for the zebra bag
- 4 medium stencil brushes for the giraffe bag
- 1.7 m black webbing, 2 cm wide, cut in two for each bag

10 Apply terracotta paint over the yellow, working in a larger circle to allow a little of the yellow to show through.

11 Apply a little of the chocolate brown paint around the edges of each section and remove the border stencil. Reposition and continue until the border is complete along the top of the bag.

12 Position the giraffe and use the same colour combination as that used for the border to stencil the entire animal. By leaving lighter sections on the haunches and shoulder of the giraffe, a more life-like result is obtained.

13 Stencil in the grass with olive fabric paint. Cure the fabric paint when dry.

TO MAKE UP · TO MAKE UP · TO MAKE UP · TO MAKE UP

1 Fold the bag with the printed side to the inside and stitch the side seam. A French seam will give you a stronger seam.

2 Sew the short sides of the extended bottom section to the main body of the bag, to form the sides, then sew the long side of the extension to the remaining bottom edge.

3 Turn the bag right side out.

4 Pin the webbing in position to form handles and stitch securely.

5 Trim any loose threads and you're ready to shop.

CUTTING INSTRUCTIONS FOR SHOPPING BAG

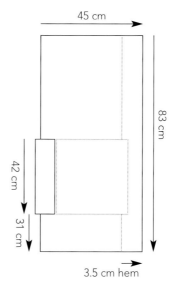

45 cm

83 cm

42 cm

31 cm

3.5 cm hem

PLASTIC SHOWER CURTAIN

Although most modern showers have glass doors, there are many showers in older houses and holiday homes with curtains in need of replacement. Just for fun, I have used a clear plastic here – an opaque, pastel-coloured plastic would work just as well. The same concept may be used to print on plastic for cosmetic bags and other purposes. Be sure to work in a well-ventilated area.

YOU WILL NEED

- adhesive spray
- newspaper
- masking tape
- 2 m glass clear plastic, 400 μ thick (a lighter-weight plastic may be used as long as it bends and drapes well)
- aerosol spray paints in the following colours: machinery grey, cream, sky blue, azure blue, pink
- cardboard – pieces from an old box will do
- curtain tape
- hooks to hang curtain

1 Size the four sea life stencils on a photocopier and cut the stencils.

2 Spray the back of each stencil with adhesive spray.

3 Using old newspaper and some masking tape, tape a frame around each stencil.

4 Plan the position of the designs on the plastic and secure the stencils.

5 Shake the aerosol paints very well for at least a minute, then spray a few bursts onto newspaper before printing. Give the cans a little shake each time again before using.

6 I first used a light base coat of cream on each stencil to create an opaque layer for the other colours on which to 'sit'.

7 Combine the colours by giving a gentle spray to each stencil from different angles, holding a piece of cardboard in front to direct the spray. The last colour will be most prominent.

8 Remove the stencils and leave them to dry completely before repositioning. Repeat until the whole curtain is finished.

TO MAKE UP • TO MAKE UP

1 Cut the plastic to the required length allowing for a small hem at the top.

2 Sew on the curtain tape.

3 Thread through the hooks and hang the curtain. There is no need for a bottom hem unless you want added weight.

COTTON DHURRIE BATHMAT

These small, fringed mats make super bathmats or little bedside rugs and, being 100% cotton, take fabric paints very well. To heat-cure, I recommend the oven or tumbledrier method, as ironing will not heat the heavily textured fabric enough to cure the fabric paints.

YOU WILL NEED

- cotton dhurrie mat
- fabric paints in faded denim and flesh
- 2 medium stencil brushes

1 I used the same sea life motifs as were used on the shower curtain (see photograph on page 81), and printed it on both sides of the mat.

2 Fabric paint in faded denim and flesh is blended into the sea creatures in the same manner as for the shower curtain.

3 You will find that much effort is required to work the paint into the heavily textured fabric and you will definitely need more paint than usual to achieve a good, clear print.

4 The designs that were used for the shower curtain were scattered over the rest of the mat and I cut out a simple starfish and yacht outline to fill in any spaces that looked bare.

5 Heat-cure the paint in an oven or tumbledrier.

VOILE BATHROOM CURTAIN

To add the final finishing touch to the bathroom, I resized the sea motifs once again and sprayed them onto voile for delicate curtains – a lovely contrast to the cotton dhurrie bathmat.

YOU WILL NEED

- adhesive spray
- newspaper
- masking tape
- voile, enough to make up curtains to required size
- aerosol spray paints in the following colours: machinery grey, sky blue, azure blue, pink
- cardboard – pieces from an old box will do
- curtain tape
- curtain hooks (suitable for tape)

1 On a photocopier, enlarge the motifs to the size you want – I sized up each on an A5 sheet of paper.

2 Cut the stencils and spray the back of each with adhesive spray.

3 Using newspaper and masking tape, tape a frame around each stencil. Decide on the position of your designs and secure the stencils in place.

4 Shake the aerosol paints very well and spray a few bursts onto spare newspaper before starting to print. Combine the colours by giving each stencil a gentle spray of each colour of your choice, using a piece of cardboard as a shield to prevent the spray from spreading, and to 'bounce' it back onto the fabric.

5 Remove the stencils and reposition. Repeat until the entire curtain is complete.

TO MAKE UP · TO MAKE UP

1 Make a small fold at the top of the curtain and sew on the curtain tape.

2 Hem the bottom edges.

3 Thread through the hooks and hang.

MOSAIC GECKO STEPS

I have always loved the way that the Spanish and other European cultures embellish the risers (the upright part of a step) in a flight of stairs, usually with tiles. Risers seem to be such a nondescript part of a building to want to decorate, but when complete – what a difference!

When I painted my own front steps with a mock tile finish, I decided to include geckos as there are always so many of these little creatures around and I thought they would be a fitting motif for the risers. I also included a traditional good luck design border from the Ashanti people of Ghana – said to be a charm against negative influences – to protect my home.

Although I had a very definite idea of what I wanted to achieve, I drew a scale plan to try different tile designs and to gain a better mind picture of the final result before I started. The steps in question are the entrance steps to a very old house and there were quite a number of cracks to fill. Nevertheless, the working surface still presented many bumps and uneven plaster.

TILES • TILES • TILES • TILES • TILES

1 Clean and prepare the cement surface before applying two coats of a good quality exterior PVA. This not only provides the base coat, but will also form the grouting between the tiles. If you are working on an old cement surface, it is advisable to apply binding liquid, after scrubbing down the area thoroughly. In the case of newly laid cement, you will have to ask your hardware shop dealer for advice because the cement needs a period of time to cure before paint may be applied.

2 Cut to size a stencil template of an octagonal floor tile, as well as another smaller square tile. Use them to mark, in pencil, the position of the 'tiles' on the floor. Don't be concerned about the pencil marks as they will be completely covered by the paint as you stencil, eliminating the need to rub them out.

3 First set aside approximately one cup of scumble glaze and mix it with one tablespoon of green universal stainer. Mix half the remaining scumble glaze with two tablespoons of red oxide universal stainer, and the rest of the scumble glaze with two tablespoons of brown universal stainer.

4 Make up two fairly large foam sponges, and another smaller sponge, as described in the chapter on Tools and Materials on page 7.

5 Spray adhesive onto the tile templates, then position each template according to the lines you pencilled in step 2. Using red glaze, lightly sponge the larger tile, working from the sides of the tile towards the centre but always keeping the centre of the tile a few shades lighter.

6 With the brown glaze, sponge over the red tiles again, still leaving the centres lighter. Use the sponge to soften any obvious marks.

7 Remove the stencil and check that no glaze is on the back of it before repositioning for the next tile. Complete all the large tiles in this manner.

YOU WILL NEED

- 5 litres exterior PVA in stone
- binding liquid (if necessary)
- 1 litre acrylic scumble glaze
- 50 ml universal stainer in red oxide, green and brown
- 3 sponges
- adhesive spray
- 3 small stencil brushes
- fabric paints in hunter's green and maroon
- masking tape
- 50 ml water-based copper-coloured paint
- black liner, if required
- 5 litres sealant recommended by your hardware dealer

8 Use the green glaze to sponge the smaller tiles – two coats might be necessary to obtain the density of colour required. Again, keep the centre of the tiles slightly lighter.

9 When the paint is dry, rub out any visible pencil lines with a rubber and neaten any edges of the grouting lines with base coat and a small flat brush.

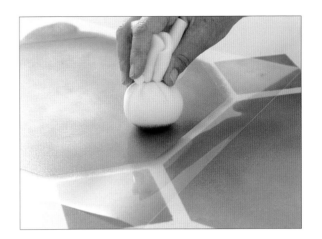

MOSAICS · MOSAICS · MOSAICS · MOSAICS · MOSAICS

1 Photocopy the Ashanti border design and the mosaic gecko stencil at the back of the book to size – I allowed 1-cm squares for the tiles. Cut the geckos on a separate stencil from the surrounding tile design as it is quicker to paint them individually. You may have to trim the surrounding edges to fit the areas on which you are working.

2 Spray the back of the Ashanti border stencil with adhesive spray and attach masking tape to the top edge of the step for additional hold, if necessary. Stencil the border with a small stencil brush and maroon paint at the top of the riser.

3 With hunter's green and a small stencil brush or a small sponge, stencil the tiles that surround the gecko design below the completed Ashanti border.

4 Use the copper paint to stencil the geckos, placing them carefully in the open spaces of the tile design. If desired, a black liner can be used to emphasise the eyes.

5 Paint the lower Ashanti border to complete.

6 Allow all paint to dry completely before applying four coats of the recommended sealant to protect the surfaces. Allow each coat to dry thoroughly between applications and ensure that the area is dust free before applying another layer of paint.

KITCHEN FLOOR MOSAIC

This was the first cement floor that I attempted and I decided to go for quite a complicated, tiled design using a border of mosaic stencilling to break up the area. The result was beautiful and I was really taken aback at how simple it was to achieve. It was also fairly quick to complete. I spent far more time removing the tatty linoleum from the floor, after which the glue that had been used to stick it down had to be dissolved and scraped off using paint thinners – an awful, smelly job! The painting itself only took two days.

I was working on quite an old floor that had a fair number of cracks and bumps but decided that, in keeping with the age of the house, I would work with this and only fill in some of the more obvious cracks with a masonry patching plaster. Two coats of PVA were applied to create a good working base, and which would also form the 'grouting' between the painted tiles.

Using the measurements of a floor tile, the kitchen was marked out in pencil and masking tape stuck down to form the tiles. In retrospect I would not mark in pencil as it took ages to rub the marks out once I had finished – just measure and apply the masking tape in one go but you will need someone to help you with this.

Once the design was all taped out, I applied the first glaze – universal stainers in red oxide mixed in a water-based glaze. I worked the glaze onto the marked tiles in a circular motion with a bathroom sponge torn in two, leaving the centre of each tile a little lighter. The glaze dries very quickly and the movement of the sponge leaves lovely swirly marks on the floor. However, when I completed the red glaze and looked at the floor, the colour looked awful – garish and definitely not the old terracotta look I had imagined! A quick trip to the hardware shop for more glaze and some brown universal stainers later and bingo! The brown glaze toned down the red and immediately gave the impression of old tiles. The magic of colour blending never fails to impress me.

The mosaic stencil was then applied in the borders in two layers – the leaves and berries first, using a fabric paint, and then the cream tesserae or tiles, using a cream PVA. The stencil was sprayed with adhesive and the paint applied with brushes. Small corner motifs repeated the main design and formed neat turning points.

Once I had removed the masking tape and rubbed out the pencil lines, I had quite a bit of tidying up to do as the glaze had leaked under the masking tape but a little paint and a steady hand soon fixed that. Masking tape must be removed quite quickly, otherwise it becomes quite attached to the surface and pulls the basecoat off when it is removed. I have found on subsequent floors that if I stencil the tiles using a template, it reduces the amount of patching up afterwards. Two coats of hardwearing sealer were applied and I had an extremely practical, unique kitchen floor that just needed a mop down to keep clean.

I made matching curtains from a bleached, cream cotton twill fabric and used the leaf and berry motif stencilled in the same fabric paint colours as used on the floor. I reversed the border on the bottom of the curtains so that it would match up when closed.

As an indication of cost, the kitchen measures roughly 7 x 5 m and all the materials came to about R500.00. At the time, a new linoleum floor would have set me back at least R3 000.00, but apart from the saving I have a unique floor with loads of character!

BERRY NOTEPAPER AND MATCHING ENVELOPE

It is simple to make your own personalised writing paper with envelopes to match. For an envelope template, open up a standard envelope in the size you require. Trace around the envelope and mark where the fold lines are situated. Cut this shape out of stencil material, creating slits so that you can mark the fold lines in pencil.

Use this template as a pattern to draw around, on paper of your choice, also marking the position of the folds in pencil through the slits in the template. Fold up as per the original envelope and glue the sides.

1 Make three photocopies of the section of the Berries and Cherries design (at the back of the book) to the size you require.

2 Secure each copy to a sheet of stencil material and number the front of each sheet '1', '2' or '3' with a felt-tip pen in the top right-hand corner. Cut out all the areas marked '1' on the first sheet, remembering to cut on the outside of the lines and to cut the four registration points. Repeat for sheets 2 and 3. Remove the paper copies.

3 Spray the back of your stencil *very* lightly with adhesive spray. Wait a few seconds for it to dry, then press against a soft fabric (a T-shirt is ideal, as it will not leave any marks). This will remove any excess stickiness so that it does not adhere permanently to the paper.

4 Gently press stencil 1 in the chosen position over the art paper.

5 Tape up your stencil brushes with masking tape so that only about 5 mm of the bristles protrude – to prevent paint from seeping under the stencil.

6 Apply red fabric paint to the areas of the fruit on stencil 1, leaving a small section of light in the centre of each fruit. Stencil around the edge of each fruit with maroon. Pick up tiny quantities of paint with your brush and work off any excess on newspaper if necessary, then apply to your stencil. Do not wet the paper too much with paint or it will distort when dry.

7 Softly stencil the leaves with olive green, then edge with hunter's green and use a plastic shield to create the vein down the centre of each leaf.

8 Repeat with leaves and fruit on stencils 2 and 3.

9 Apply 3D paint to form the seeds of strawberries, if desired, or else stencil with chocolate brown fabric paint.

10 Stencil the envelope to match.

YOU WILL NEED

- glue stick
- adhesive spray
- 2 A4 sheets of matching paper (weight of 130 g should be sufficient)
- 5 small stencil brushes
- masking tape
- fabric paints in red, maroon, olive, hunter's green and chocolate brown
- 3D paint (if required)

BLIND EMBOSSED CARD

Use good quality paper when making cards. For instance, for a 'thank you' card I used a smart navy paper with embossed gold lettering for a stylish touch. A precise cut is important, so either use a rotary guillotine or ask a printing shop to cut the card for you.

YOU WILL NEED

- A4 artist's card
- embossing tool or a fine knitting needle
- cream paint or embossing powder in gold

1 Choose a font for your lettering that suits the type of card you wish to make. Computers are invaluable for this as they have such a large range of fonts and you can see exactly what they will look like, size them correctly and print a copy immediately for cutting. For my 'thank you' card, I wanted a very smart card for a formal occasion so I chose a font called Parchment, which has many swirls and curlicues.

2 Attach the print of the lettering to a sheet of stencil material and cut your stencil – make sure that all letters with closed loops have bridges in them.

3 Cut your card to size – I simply cut the A4 card in half and then folded it into a card.

4 Position your stencil on the front of the card and secure with four small pieces of masking tape.

5 Use the embossing tool to rub over the card from the inside. It will soon become apparent where the stencil openings are and you can then follow the lines.

6 Once you have finished embossing, remove the stencil and spray the back very lightly with adhesive.

7 Reattach the stencil to the card and apply gold paint or ink as well as embossing powder through the stencil.

8 Remove the stencil.

MARINE LIFE WASTE BIN

Many of the craft shops sell 'blanks', which are wooden, finely finished products suitable for decoration. These are ideal for stencilling and make lovely customised gifts and saleable articles. For this project I have used a waste bin with generous proportions and given it a 'beach house' feel using delicate seahorse stencils with a touch of gold to add interest.

1　Paint the waste bin with one coat of universal undercoat, both inside and out. Leave to dry overnight.

2　Paint the entire bin with one coat of white PVA. For a really smooth finish on the outside, roll over the paint with a sponge roller – this will also give the paint technique a good final finish. Leave to dry.

3　Tape a strip of masking tape around the top of the waste bin.

4　Apply a light coat of PVA in azure below the tape. Then, using a soft rag, gently dab the paint until all brush marks disappear.

5　Mix about 1 teaspoon of faded denim fabric paint with $1/2$ cup of water and apply with a soft rag until softly blended. Remove the masking tape immediately and leave to dry.

6　Photocopy the required stencils from the back of the book to the desired size. (I used the wave border with a width of 1 cm, the small seahorse in the rope frame to a height of 13 cm and the large seahorse to a height of 16 cm.)

7　Attach each of the copies to sheets of stencil material, then cut out the stencils.

8　Spray the backs of the stencils lightly with adhesive spray.

9　Position the wave border on the line between the white and painted areas of the waste bin and, using a medium stencil brush, stencil with navy fabric paint.

YOU WILL NEED

- 2.5 mm paintbrush
- waste bin 'blank'
- universal undercoat paint
- PVA in white and azure
- small sponge roller
- 1.5 cm masking tape
- piece of soft rag
- fabric paints in faded denim and navy
- spray adhesive
- 2 medium stencil brushes
- oil-based cream paint in gold
- 1 small stencil brush
- gold felt tipped pen with 'V' cut into nib
- water-based glaze in gloss finish

10 It is easier to work on the surface if the bin is lying flat. However, remember to leave the paint to dry before moving on to the next section.

11 Place the stencil of the large seahorse in the middle of the panel and stencil, using a medium stencil brush with faded denim fabric paint.

12 Shade the outer areas of the stencil in navy. The little shell may be stencilled in gold cream paint with a small brush for added interest.

13 On the next panel, stencil the wave border, ensuring that the pattern in the corner correctly meets the previous border.

14 Secure the small seahorse stencil in the rope frame in the centre of the panel and apply gold cream paint to the rope circle.

15 Stencil the seahorse in faded denim and navy as before.

16 Repeat the design for the next two panels.

17 Using a gold-coloured felt pen, run a line around the upper edge of the waste bin.

18 As the cream paint is oil-based, it will take approximately ten days to dry completely before you can apply a coat of water-based glaze to seal.

CUPBOARD DOORS

A small stencil detail on an uninteresting piece of furniture can turn it into a collector's item. The rather unexciting cupboard doors pictured here had an attractive moulded frame that cried out for a bit of decoration. The doors were painted with a white thixotropic or gel-like paint as this provides a satiny finish and is easy to wipe off dirty fingerprints, etc. The paint is also easy to apply, as unlike many oil-based enamels, it does not run.

I first removed the little wooden knobs to give them a miniature stencil detail and to paint them in a contrasting colour. A sage green PVA was thinned down with water – about four tablespoons of PVA to half a cup of water – and then washed over the white paint. I dried the brush on paper to remove most of the paint and then slowly dragged the brush through the paint, wiping the excess paint off at the end of each stroke. This created a softly textured background for the stencilling, which was painted with fabric paints using an opaque white for the daisies. The wooden knobs were painted with undiluted sage paint and stencilled with a tiny daisy stencil, just big enough to fit the centre of the knob.

The same technique was used for a cupboard with the lavender pots design, but here I painted the wooden moulding in a contrasting colour and used a lavender PVA for the dragging wash.

One coat of a matt-finish, water-based glaze will protect the stencilling and also enhances the colours. The cupboard doors can simply be wiped down with a damp cloth to remove dust and dirty marks.

DADO BORDER FOR WALLS

For this project I used a nasturtium design as a border for a dado. Framing it between softly coloured, moulded wooden strips creates a striking feature in the room.

Although exactly the same fabric paints and colours are used as for the nasturtium cushion (see page 66), the colours are somewhat subdued when painted over a PVA background, which is preferable as it would otherwise look too harsh. However, the design still looks cheerful and cosy. The wall has been colour-washed in a diluted PVA, rich cream shade, while the bottom half has had a wash of watered-down PVA in pumpkin, gently rubbed on with a soft cloth.

1 Decide on the width of the border and mark it in pencil right around the room at the desired height.

2 If you want a contrasting colour or a paint effect for the background of your stencil, do this now. Be careful not to go too far over the pencil lines.

3 Follow the instructions for the nasturtium cushion from steps 3 to 6 (see page 68).

4 Position your stencil precisely between the pencil lines that have been marked out, then mark the registration points lightly in pencil.

YOU WILL NEED

- Plascon Polvin™ in cream and pumpkin
- fabric paints in each of the following colours: light yellow, mustard, orange, olive green, hunter's green
- 4 small stencil brushes
- 1 medium stencil brush
- water-based glaze in a matt finish (optional)
- moulded wood strips
- silicone or No More Nails™

5 Refer to the design pattern to see which parts of the stencil are flowers and which parts are leaves.

6 Using a small stencil brush, apply light yellow to all flowers. Apply mustard to the edges of the flowers followed by a very light touch of orange.

7 With a medium stencil brush, cover the stems and leaves with olive green paint, not forgetting to leave a lighter area in the centre of the leaves. Outline each leaf with a little hunter's green. Remove stencil 1.

8 Use the same set of registration marks to position stencil 2, then print the leaves, flowers and stems as described in steps 4 and 5. Apply hunter's green to the leaf veins. Remove stencil 2.

9 Position stencil 3 with the aid of the registration marks and complete as before, applying hunter's green to the seedpods. Remove stencil 3.

10 Position stencil 4 as previously and apply mustard, followed by a touch of orange to the flower detail and olive green to the remaining stem. Remove stencil 4.

11 Secure stencil 1 to the right of the completed design aligning the two righthand registration marks with the holes in the left of the stencil and pencilling in another two marks in the righthand registration holes.

12 When the border is complete, erase all the registration marks.

13 If you wish, one coat of a matt-finish glaze may be applied to protect the stencilling.

14 Select one of the colours from the stencilled border, or a contrasting colour, and paint the moulded wooden strips. Fix into position with silicone or No More Nails™ to cover the pencil lines.

15 Cut mitred corners to fit around the wall corners.

CAPE DUTCH WALL FRIEZE

Examples of late 18th century wall friezes can be seen today in some of the manor houses in the Western Cape, where it was quite common for travelling artisans to decorate the walls of homes and public buildings. As more farmers became established in the interior of the country, the artisans and their work followed and so the frieze fashion moved further afield.

The brief for the design featured here was for a stencil design in keeping with the age and style of the hotel, which was being restored at the time. The client liked the look of the wall friezes used in many of the old Cape Dutch homesteads and a simple stencil along those lines was designed. The colours were chosen to complement the furnishings and curtains, and the paints were sponged onto the wall. The stencil was placed in the traditional Cape Dutch manner, optically splitting the wall and visually reducing the height of the room, and framing the architectural points of interest such as doors and fanlights. The final effect was to draw the various seating areas of this vast room together and add warmth and charm.

1 Photocopy the Cape Dutch stencil design at the back of the book to the required size.

2 Secure the copy to the stencil material and cut out the design – you may want to add extra bridges to the border lines or paint them in separately afterwards as the stencil can become hard to work with if long lines are cut out.

3 Measure and mark the position of the frieze on the wall in pencil in order to ensure that your stencil runs straight.

4 Lightly spray the back of the stencil with adhesive. Masking tape may also be helpful to keep the stencil in position.

5 Sponge all areas of the stencil very softly with olive green and apply rust to the tips of the berries.

YOU WILL NEED

- adhesive spray
- masking tape (if required)
- sponges
- PVA paint in shades of rust and olive green

COUNTRY KITCHEN BORDER

The basis for this design was a much-loved, beautiful curtain fabric of ferns, daisies and other periwinkle blue flowers. The client wanted elements from the curtain design repeated around the walls to form a loose border. The end result added light and airiness to quite a dark kitchen and, by applying the stencil just beneath the ceiling cornice, added height and interest to the room.

To design the stencil, I used a piece of the fabric and photocopied it. Once I had decided which elements to use I drew these in a border, but simplifying them slightly. I decided on a two-layered stencil that would create the desired effect without becoming too finicky, after which I added smaller details with liners and pens.

Because the wall surface was well prepared and smooth to work on, I used a combination of fabric paints and PVA.

CHILD'S CUP AND BOWL SET

This ceramic cup and bowl set makes use of a simple but delightful animal design and bright colours that will appeal to a young child. The leopard stencil is cut in two parts, while the raised spots (achieved with the use of a 3D paint) provide an interesting texture for small fingers.

1 Paint the inside of the cup and bowl in yellow-orange using a China brush.

2 Run a line of mahogany around the rim of the cup and bowl with a sponge.

3 Photocopy your stencil design to the desired size and cut the stencils directly from the paper. You will need an extremely sharp blade to achieve a clean cut.

4 With a sponge, dampen the article you want to stencil.

5 Position the first stencil and wet the paper thoroughly until it sticks to the curves of the bisque blank and is in close contact with it. The blank will absorb water very quickly so it may be necessary to wet the paper a number of times.

6 With your stencilling sponge apply the mahogany underglaze to the leopard outline stencil.

7 Position the second stencil to fill in the body sections left open by the first stencil, then apply the orange underglaze paint with a sponge.

8 Remove the stencil and neaten any uneven edges with a sharp tool, if necessary.

9 Use the reinforcement stickers as templates to create colourful dots on the cup and bowl.

10 I used a 3D underglaze in the centre of the dots and for the leopard's spots, to create textural interest.

11 A 'harden on' firing will show up any further areas that need neatening with a sharp tool.

12 Lead-free glaze is applied before the final firing.

YOU WILL NEED

- bisque cup and bowl blanks
- underglaze paints in mahogany, orange and yellow orange
- China brush
- 2 small sponges
- water
- file reinforcement stickers (available from stationery shops)
- ceramic underglaze paint (3D effect) in brown
- lead-free glaze

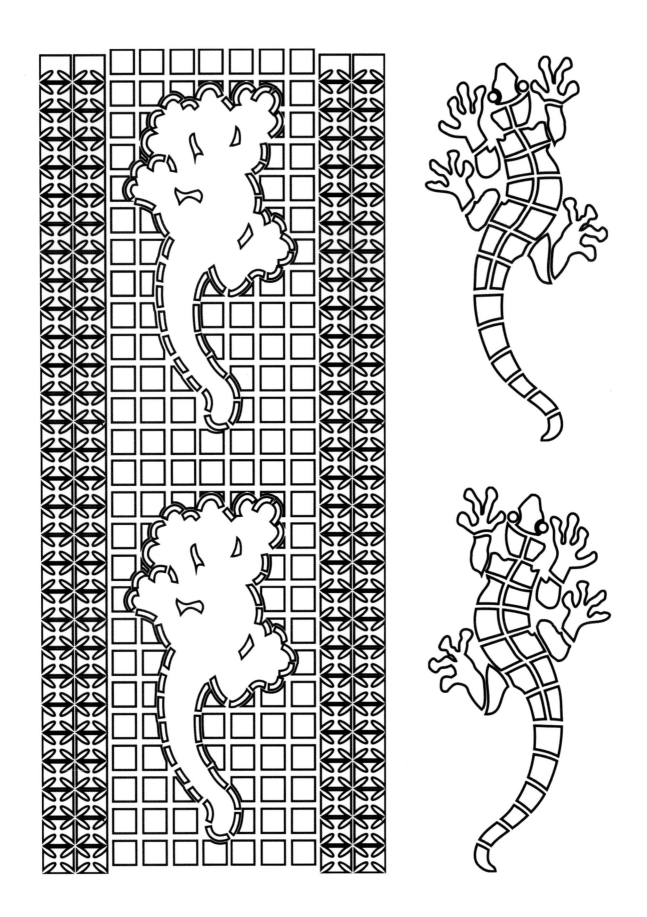

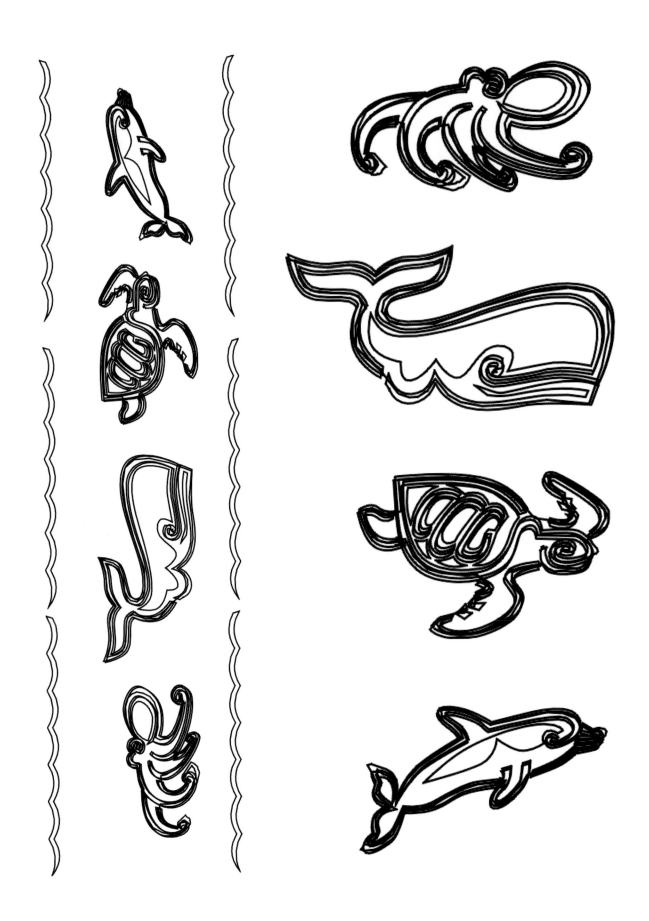

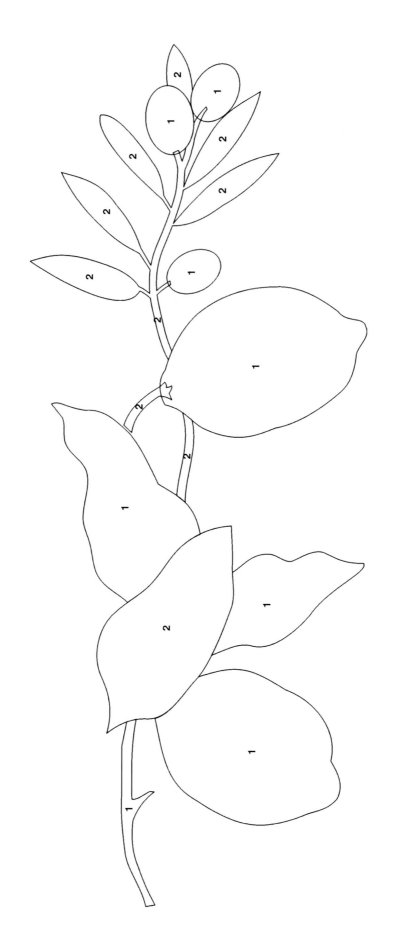

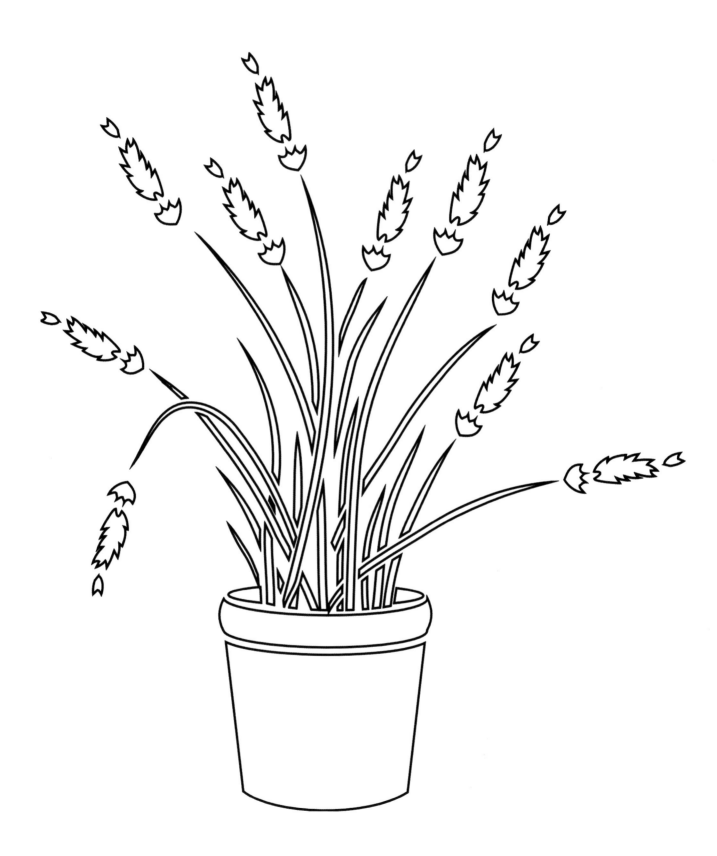

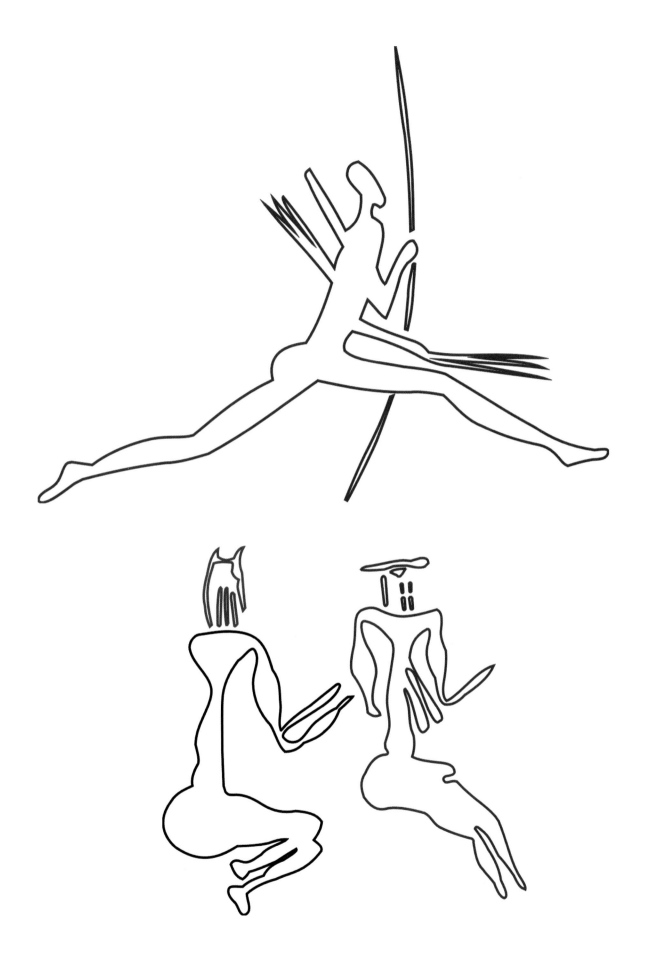

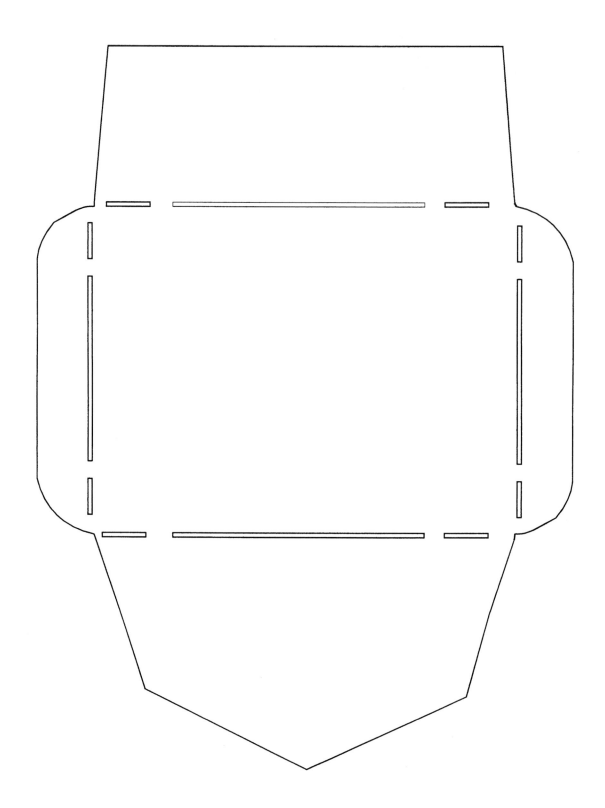

SUPPLIERS

NATIONAL

The following suppliers either have branches countrywide or they may be contacted for information on outlets throughout the country that stock their products.

Crisitex Fabric Paints
PO Box 12400
Clubview
0069
Tel: 012 6536853
Fabric paints

Mica Hardware
Branches countrywide
Genkem aerosol adhesive spray

Plascon Paints
Private Bag X4010
Kenmare
1745
Tel: 011 9552161
General paints, aerosol paints, glazes and varnish

Waltons Stationery Co
Branches countrywide
Stencil material, cutting boards and knives

GAUTENG

Herbert Evans Art Shop
Shop 21 Galleria Centre
Cnr Bierman and Cradock Avenue
Rosebank
2196
Tel: 011 447 3262
Stencil cream paints

Home Hyper City
19 Pretorius Street
Pretoria (Tshwane)
0002
Tel: 012 323 7860
Hopsack linen, bull denim and canvas

JMD
5 Perskor Park
Richards Drive
Halfway House
1682
Tel:011 315 3323
Ceramic blanks

Uniquely Yours
Shop 19 Rock Cottage Shopping Centre
Cnr John Vortser and Christiaan
De Wet Road
Weltevreden Park (ext 82)
1709
Tel: 011 794 2488
Ceramic blanks, paints and tools

KWAZULU-NATAL

Classic Textiles
1st floor,
126 Archary Rd (Opp Makro)
Clairwood
4052
Tel:031 465 9016
Hopsack linen and bull denim

Pavillion Stationers
7 Pavillion Centre
Westville
3630
Tel: 031 265 0760
Stencil cream paints

Purple Hippo Creations
8 Stedman Mews
128 Jan Hofmeyr Road
Westville
3630
Tel: 031 266 9416
Ceramic blanks

SA Canvas
401 North Coast Road
Briardene
4051
Tel: 031 564 2365
Canvas

WESTERN CAPE

Cape Pottery Supplies
PO Box 36
Steenberg
7947
Tel: 021 7011320
Ceramic blanks

Crafter's Inn
Shop 9
Morkel's Arcade
Caledon Street
Somerset West
7130
Tel: 021 8515299
DecoArt stencil cream paints

Outline Stencils
PO Box 842
Somerset West
7129
Tel: 021 8524359/8529642
Stencils, stencil brushes and all the pre-cut designs used in this book

S A Canvas
PO Box 61
Maitland
7404
Tel: 021 5118989
Canvas

SBH Cotton Mills
Evans Avenue
Epping Industria
7460
Tel: 021 5344431
Hopsack linen and bull denim fabric

INDEX

Italicised page numbers indicate illustrations